THE HOST
WITH THE MOST

When Alfred Hitchcock invites you to a party, you can be sure to meet the most interesting people.

That seductive girl who smiles at you has the most sensuous style in slipping that funny white powder into your drink.

That big hearty fellow who pounds you warmly on the back has a hand that's very handy in handling cold steel.

That distinguished gentleman with a custom tailored suit has a cunning pocket sewn in for his special order pistol.

They may not exactly be the Beautiful People, but they'll go all out to give you the time of your life— as long as your life lasts, that is. . . .

COFFIN BREAK

COFFIN BREAK

ALFRED HITCHCOCK,
Editor

A DELL BOOK

Published by
Dell Publishing Co., Inc.
1 Dag Hammarskjold Plaza
New York, New York 10017
Copyright © 1974 by H.S.D. Publications, Inc.

CONTENTS

INTRODUCTION
by Alfred Hitchcock

My friend Frockton complained to me recently about inefficiency. Not his own, you may be sure. This particular inefficiency had been committed by a mail-order nursery. What eventually became a harrowing experience for Frockton began when he sent in an order for a hedge. What he got instead was a shipment of full-blooming asters large enough to enable him to plant the entire state of Rhode Island. Once an absurdity like that begins, of course, there's no putting an end to it. Frockton's letters of indignation to the nursery produced not the hedge he so coveted but additional shipments of unwanted flora. When the affair finally petered out—with Frockton's surrender—he was up to his asters in honeysuckle vines, heliopsis and azaleas.

I mention Frockton's complaint because it gives me the opportunity to promote one of my most cherished beliefs. That is, that inefficiency, far from being a curse, is one of mankind's most glorious blessings. The explanation is quite simple. Inefficiency keeps people gainfully occupied who otherwise would be getting into all sorts of mischief. The alternative to inefficiency, I am convinced, is mass unemployment.

Consider Frockton's case. Assume that all had gone according to plan. An employee at the nursery receives Frockton's order, fills it and sends it off. One person is productively employed for, at the most, ten minutes. Efficiency has been served. But to what end? Man has become an automaton for no better purpose than Frockton's getting his hedge prior to the first killing frost.

For contrast, let's speculate on what actually happened. Employee Number One receives Frockton's order. He is at the moment diagramming a Split T formation for a fellow gridiron enthusiast, Employee Number Two, and he uses Frockton's order to represent a tackle. In the ensuing clash between the opposing teams, a number of orders are—shall we say?—fractured, among them Frockton's. When reassembled they are not quite as they were. Consequently, a gentleman in Utah receives Frockton's hedge, and Frockton, as we already know, is the recipient of the Utah gentleman's asters.

A minor tragedy for Utah and Frockton. But for mankind, I insist, a small step forward. In place of one employee, two have been actively engaged. And, perhaps best of all, a full hour and a quarter of man's embarrassing surplus of time has been consumed.

In due time, the mail order nursery's Employee Number Three, whose duty it is to respond to irate customers' complaints, receives Frockton's letter. He contacts Employee Number One, who immediately calls in Employee Number Two as a consultant. Working together the three locate the cause of the error. The many orders are dissected, then put back together once more. Since all the pieces appear to fit it is assumed that the mistake has been remedied. Frockton's hedge is quickly dispatched—to a lady in Ohio—and the gentleman in Utah is sent a form letter of apology, along with a carload of blue spruce. And, as we know, a bundle of the best honeysuckle goes off to Frockton.

Three employees have now become involved in this worthy endeavor and an additional day that otherwise would have lain fallow has been constructively put to use.

It takes no imagination whatsoever to guess how it came to pass that Frockton was eventually sent the heliopsis and azaleas—and surprised lady and gentleman gardeners all across the land found Frockton's hedges in their morning mail. It can be assumed that when Frockton's second letter of discontent arrived at the nursery, the organization's middle-level management team was drawn into the act. Time-and-motion studies were initiated, performed by Employees Four-through-Eleven. Employees Twelve-through-Nineteen were detailed to form a counter-intelligence unit to investigate the possibility that the "errors" were the result of espionage.

And, of course, when Frockton's third letter arrived a crisis was declared. Top-level management took over. Soon, a complete middle-to-bottom reorganization was begun, the main thrust of which was to move the water cooler three paces to the west.

Thus, thanks to inefficiency, countless employees were kept busy for a period of months. It all proves quite neatly, I believe, that in a world plagued by gross overpopulation, no amount of bungling can ever be enough.

Fortunately or unfortunately, depending on your point of view, not one iota of inefficiency will be found in the pages that follow. Our authors have made certain that every story comes out exactly even at The End.

A GIRL MUST BE PRACTICAL

by Richard Deming

The phone call Lydia Hartman had been awaiting all day came just as she was leaving the office. She paused in the doorway and waited to see if it was for her.

She heard her boss say, "Apex Insurance. Mr. Tremaine speaking." Then he looked up and motioned toward her energetically.

Crossing the room, she took the phone from Tremaine's hand and said into it, "Mrs. Hartman speaking."

"This is Jules," a deep masculine voice said in her ear. "I'm calling from Buffalo."

"Buffalo!" she said abruptly.

"You told me to stick with him no matter where he went," Jules Weygand said a trifle resentfully. "When he caught a bus to Buffalo, I drove my car up and was waiting at the depot here when he arrived."

Lydia glanced toward her boss, who had moved across the room and was lifting his hat from a clothes tree.

"Does he know you followed him?" she asked in a low voice.

"He hasn't seen me. I feel like a private eye, tailing him around like this from one city to the next."

From the doorway Mr. Tremaine said, " 'Night, Lydia. Lock the door when you leave, will you?"

Placing her hand over the mouth piece, Lydia said, "All right, Mr. Tremaine. Good-night."

Then, as the door closed behind her boss, she said into the phone, "Is he all right?"

"Of course he's all right," Weygand said with a shade more resentment. "He's registered at the Redmill Hotel, and since noon he's had two pints of bourbon delivered. I told you he wasn't planning anything but a drunk."

"Oh, my!" she said. "If he's drunk, he might do anything. I'm coming there."

"I thought you probably would," he said resignedly. "So I checked train and bus schedules. The next train leaves Rochester at six P.M. and gets here at seven-thirty. There isn't a bus leaving there until eight."

"I'll be on the next train."

"What do you expect to accomplish?" he asked.

"I might prevent him from doing something desperate, Jules."

"Like killing himself? Drunks don't commit suicide."

"Jim's hardly a drunk," she said sharply. "You can't blame him for going off the deep end after losing everything he had."

"He lost it for me too," Weygand said dryly. "I was his partner, remember?"

"I know," she said on a note of contrition. "You've been like the Rock of Gibralter in this, Jules. You could have prosecuted."

"I didn't hold off for his sake, Lydia. Only for yours. You know how I feel about you."

"I don't want to hear that as long as I'm married to Jim," she said with a return of sharpness. "And I certainly can't leave him now, when he needs me more than he ever has."

"That sounds as though you finally plan to, once he's straightened out," Weygand said in a pleased voice. "It's the first real encouragement you've given me."

"Meet me at the station at seven-thirty," she said, and hung up.

Jules Weygand was waiting when Lydia Hartman got off the train at Buffalo. When she saw him standing, tall and lean and handsome, at the top of the inclined ramp leading up from the trains, it occurred to her that a month ago the sight would have made her heart skip a beat. But then he had been a successful business-man; now he was a bankrupt. She might have traded one successful businessman for another, but she had no desire to trade a bankrupt for a bankrupt. At thirty-two a girl had to start being practical.

He stood smiling down at her as she moved upward toward him, openly admiring the rounded slimness of her body. When she paused before him and he took the small overnight bag from her hand, she tossed her blond head pettishly.

"You shouldn't look at me like that," she said.

"You shouldn't be so beautiful," he countered, taking her elbow to steer her toward the main exit.

His car was parked on the lot only a few yards from the exit. Dropping the overnight bag in back, he held the door for her, then rounded the car to slide under the wheel.

Without turning on the ignition, he said, "Now that you're here, what are your plans?"

"To talk to him. If he won't come home, I'll stay here with him."

"And watch him drink himself into a stupor? He may stay on this a week."

"Then I'll stay a week."

"You'll lose your job."

"I can phone in the morning. Mr. Tremaine is understanding."

"But you've only been there three weeks, Lydia. Even an understanding boss won't put up with you taking a week off so soon."

"I'm not exactly a new employee," she said. "I worked for Apex Insurance five years while Jim was getting on his feet."

"You've been away five years too."

"Apparently I haven't been forgotten, or I wouldn't have been taken back with a set-up to chief clerk."

"Yeah," he said. "That hasn't helped Jim psychologically either, you moving back to your old employer with a promotion at the moment he's bungled himself out of business entirely."

"Bungled?"

"If embezzlement to play the ponies isn't bungling, I don't know what is. Why don't you leave him to stew in his own juice, Lydia? A month ago you were considering it."

"A month ago he wasn't down. I can't leave him now."

"Your damned loyalty," he said irritably. "He'll never get back on his feet, even if you stick with him. He's washed up."

"So I should leave him for you?" she asked sarcastically. "You're as bankrupt as he is."

"But not through my own fault. I'll spring back again, eventually. Jim won't. Even if you managed to help him back on his feet again, he'd fritter it away a second time. He's weak, Lydia."

"Perhaps. But he's my husband. And at the moment you're no better prospect than he is. I don't think you realize what a practical person I am, Jules. Even if I weren't married to Jim, I wouldn't have you at this point."

He gave her a surprised look. "Are you serious?"

"Completely," she assured him. "Maybe ten years ago I'd take the chance. As a matter of fact, I did with Jim. With youth, you don't mind helping a man struggle ahead. But I've gone through that once. Now I'm thirty-two and you're nearly forty. I'm not interested in any more financial struggles that can be avoided. I'm stuck with Jim, but I'm not about to jump from the frying pan into the fire. My next husband, if there is one, is going to be firmly established before we say the vows."

"You don't make sense," he growled. "You'll have a lot more financial struggle with Jim than you would with me."

"We happen to be already married. And I'm just as loyal as I am practical. Shall we go where he's staying?"

Wordlessly he started the engine and drove off the lot.

The Redmill Hotel was on lower Pearl Street, hardly the best section of town. However, Jules Weygand assured Lydia, it was a perfectly respectable second-class hotel. She left her overnight bag in the car when they went inside.

The building was ancient and both the furniture and carpet in the lobby were well worn, but it seemed a clean enough place. Two old men sat in the lobby reading newspapers and a middle-aged man with a bald head was behind the desk.

Going over to the desk, Weygand said to the bald man. "He still in his room swilling the booze?"

The man merely nodded. Weygand led Lydia on toward the elevator.

"I slipped him a ten to keep track of Jim's activities

for me," he said in explanation. "That's how I knew about the bourbon he had delivered."

"I'll repay all your expenses," she said.

"Don't be silly. What's a few more bucks when you're fifty thousand in the hole? I have enough ready cash."

They stepped on the elevator and Weygand said, "Seventh."

When they got off at seven, Weygand led the way down the hall and around a corner to a door numbered 714.

"Well, here you are," he said.

Over the door there was a transom with its glass painted white. It was open about four inches at the top, enough to show that a light burned in the room. Lydia gave the door a timid knock.

When there was no response, she rapped harder. After several moments of waiting, Weygand stepped forward and pounded several times.

A door across the hall opened and an elderly man peered out, then closed the door again.

Lydia said, "He must be asleep."

"More likely passed out drunk," Weygand growled. "I'll go down and have Baldy bring up a pass key."

Lydia waited in front of the door while Weygand went downstairs. In a few minutes he reappeared with the clerk.

"This is Mr. Simms, Lydia," Weygand said. "I've explained that you're Jim's wife. Mrs. Hartman, Mr. Simms."

"Pleased to meet you," the desk man said a little dubiously. "There isn't going to be any trouble here, is there?"

Lydia said, "I'm just concerned about my husband, Mr. Simms. We haven't been having any marital discord, if that's what you mean. I assure you he'll be glad to see me if you let us in."

"Well, I guess it'll be all right," Simms said reluctantly.

He fitted a pass key in the door, turned it and pushed on the knob. Nothing happened.

"He's got it bolted," Simms said. He pounded on the door until several doors along the hall opened and tenants peered out.

"Just a sound sleeper, folks," Simms announced generally. "Excuse the noise."

The tenants withdrew and their doors closed. The three in front of 714 listened for some sound within the room, but there was none.

Lydia said worriedly, "He usually snores, particularly when he's been drinking."

This made Simms look worried. He tried the pass key again, with no more result than before.

"Is there a fire escape?" Lydia asked.

Shaking his head, Simms pointed to a fire-exit sign up the hall. "Just fire stairs in each hallway. Maybe we can see something through the transom. I'll get a ladder."

He went away and was gone some ten minutes before he returned carrying a six-foot stepladder and a small, stubby screwdriver.

As he set the stepladder before the door, he said, "I know I won't be able to reach the release, because it's too far down. But I may be able to unscrew the sideplate and get the transom open that way."

Climbing the ladder, he attempted to peer into the room through the V-shaped crack left by the partially open transom.

"Can't see anything but a piece of the ceiling," he announced.

Holding the screwdriver, he thrust his right hand

through the very top of the aperture and groped around for a moment. Then he withdrew it and climbed down the ladder.

"The metal plate holding the rod that opens and closes the transom is on the right edge about halfway down," he said. "My wrist's too thick to get my hand down that far. You want to try it, lady?"

"All right," Lydia said in a steady voice.

Taking the screwdriver, she climbed the ladder. Holding the screwdriver in her left hand, she inserted her right in the crack and felt for the metal plate. As Simms had said, it was attached to the edge of the transom about halfway down. Her hand and wrist were small enough to reach it easily. She couldn't see it, but with her fingers she could feel that it was held by two screws.

Withdrawing her hand, she transferred the screwdriver to it and pushed it through the aperture again. Even though she couldn't see what she was doing, the screwdriver was short enough so that with its butt end nestled in her palm, she could still touch the screws with her fingertips. Guiding the blade into the slot of the lower screwhead, she unscrewed it, pulled her hand back out and handed the screw down to Simms.

"Better hold the top of the transom with your other hand when you unscrew the second one," Simms cautioned. "Otherwise it'll bang down against the door and maybe break the glass."

Lydia put her hand through the crack again, located the upper screw by feel and seated the blade of the screwdriver. Before unscrewing it, she grasped the top of the transom with her left hand. When the screw came all the way out, the transom was suddenly released from its rigid position. Handing down both the screw and screwdriver, Lydia cautiously let the transom move forward and swing down, climbing higher as she did and thrusting her arm farther into the room until the transom finally hung vertically downward against the door below it.

Only then did she peer through the oblong frame at the motionless figure lying on the bed. She stared at it silently for a long time.

"Is he all right?" Weygand asked.

The question roused Lydia to action. Kicking off her shoes and letting them fall to the floor, she climbed clear to the top of the ladder, steadied herself by grasping the upper part of the transom frame with both hands and slid her legs inside.

As she lowered herself to a seated position, Weygand said, "What do you think you're doing?"

"Going in to open the door," she said calmly.

Reversing herself to roll over on her stomach and transfer her grip to the bottom sill, she slid backward into the room and dropped to the floor. Quickly she crossed to the bed and bent over the still figure there.

Outside in the hall Jules Weygand tired of waiting for the door to open and climbed the ladder to peer in. His face appeared just as she turned away from the bed and began to move woodenly toward the door.

"What is it?" he asked worriedly when he saw her numb expression. He couldn't clearly see the figure on the bed because her body partially blocked the view.

Without answer she went to the door, drew back the bolt and pulled the door open. Weygand came down off the ladder, set it to one side and followed the bald-headed Simms into the room. Lydia quietly stepped out in the hall and put her shoes back on. Then she leaned against the door jamb and closed her eyes.

Inside the room the two men stared down at the figure on the bed. It was that of a man about thirty-five, good-looking in a weak sort of way, but beginning to go to fat. He wore nothing but socks and trousers, his shoes lying in one corner and the rest of his clothing wadded on top of a chair. An empty pint bottle lay next to him on the bed and another lay on the floor beside the bed. His hands were crossed on his stomach just below a thin, horizontal slit of a wound on the left side of his chest, as though he had been reaching for the wound when he died, and hadn't quite had the strength to raise his hands that high.

Simms tentatively touched the dead man's cheek, then hurriedly withdrew his hand. "Cold," he said. "Must have been dead for a while."

"And I told her drunks never commit suicide," Jules Weygand said softly.

Simms gave him a sharp look. "Suicide? Where's the knife?"

Lydia's eyes popped open. Weygand's expression turned startled. After glancing about the room, he fell on hands and knees to peer under the bed. When he rose, he stared at the desk clerk strangely.

"The door was bolted from inside," he said.

"Yeah," Simms said slowly. He glanced at the window, which was unscreened and wide open from the bottom.

"It's the seventh floor," Weygand reminded him. "And you said there's no fire escape."

He walked over to look out, then turned and stared at the closed bathroom door from narrowed eyes. Lydia's breath caught in her throat. The desk clerk gulped.

"You think the killer is still in there?" Simms whispered.

Without answering, Weygand returned to the bed, stooped and picked up the empty bottle lying next to it. Holding it by the neck, he quietly approached the bathroom door and suddenly flung it open. He stepped in with the bottle raised high as a club.

Lowering it again, he came out, his expression puzzled. Simms's gaze strayed to the door of the closet.

Striding over to it, Weygand jerked it open, the bottle again held high. The closet was empty.

With a snort of disgust Weygand set the bottle atop the dresser. Returning to the open window, he peered out a second time.

"There's a ledge about a foot wide just below the window," he announced. "Who has the rooms on either side of this one?"

"I'd have to check the register," Simms said faintly. "We'd better get out of here and let the police handle this."

"Yeah, I guess," Weygand said.

He moved toward the door. Lydia stepped back out of the way, swaying on her feet. Grasping her arm to steady her, Weygand gave her a sympathetic smile.

"I'll be all right," she said in a low voice.

Setting the spring lock, Simms pulled the door closed behind him and led the way to the elevator. Weygand steered Lydia after the desk clerk, still holding her arm. She moved stiffly, leaning against him for support.

Downstairs the two old men still sat in the lobby. Simms moved behind the desk and lifted the phone. Weygand led Lydia over to a sofa.

"I'll be all right now," she said, pulling her arm from his grip. "I don't want to sit down."

He gazed down at her speculatively. "You're sure?"

"I'm not the fainting type," she said straightening her shoulders. "I don't suppose we'll be able to go back to Rochester tonight, will we?"

"I hardly think so. The police will want to talk to us. And of course you'll have to arrange for a local funeral director to ship Jim home."

"Are you registered here?"

He shook his head. "I'm not registered anywhere. For all I knew, you meant to have me load Jim in my car and drive back to Rochester tonight. I didn't even bring a toothbrush."

"We may as well stay here, don't you think?"

"The place seems clean enough," he said with a shrug. "I'll see if I can get us a couple of rooms." He walked over to the desk just as Simms hung up the phone.

"They'll be right over," the desk clerk said. "You and Mrs. Hartman better stick around."

"We plan to," Weygand said. "Do you have a couple of rooms on the same floor, or perhaps adjoining?"

As Simms was checking his room chart, Lydia quietly walked to the door and outside. When Weygand finished registering, he turned to find her standing behind him with her overnight bag in her hand.

"You should have let me get that," he said, taking it from her.

"It isn't heavy," she said. "Did you get rooms?"

"Two right across the hall from each other on five. We may as well wait here until the police arrive, though. Mr. Simms says they'll be right along."

Lydia walked over to seat herself on the couch she had previously refused. Setting the bag next to the desk, Weygand went over to sit beside her.

A homicide team arrived five minutes later. It consisted of a burly middle-aged man who introduced himself as Sergeant Charles Carter and a lean, younger man named Harry Nicholson. Carter had a puffy, red-veined face and heavy-lidded eyes which gave a first impression of stupidity until you noted the shrewd glint in the eyes behind the drooping lids.

The first thing asked was if Simms had phoned for a doctor.

"Yes, sir," the desk clerk said. "Before I called you. We have an arrangement with a man just up the street to be on call. He should be here any minute."

"Then let's take a look at the body," Carter said. "Harry, you stay here with these folks and send the doc up when he comes."

The sergeant and Simms moved off toward the elevator.

Harry Nicholson seemed to have no intention of asking any questions about the murder, for after making a comment about the pleasant weather Buffalo was having, he lapsed into silence. Five minutes passed before a thin, elderly man carrying a medical bag came in. Nicholson walked over to meet him at the door, and after a moment's conversation the elderly man proceeded to the elevator.

Lydia glanced at her watch and was surprised to see it was only eight forty-five, just an hour and a quarter since she had gotten off the train.

Silence resumed when Nicholson returned to his seat. Apparently any questioning to be done was to be conducted by Sergeant Carter. Twenty more minutes passed before Simms, the sergeant and the doctor all got off the elevator together. The elderly doctor went out the front door. Simms and Carter came over to where Lydia, Weygand, and the other detective were seated.

"It's homicide all right," Carter informed his partner. "Somebody slid a knife between a couple of his ribs into his heart. He died so quick, he didn't even bleed. Funny thing, though."

"What's that?" Nicholson asked.

"Simms here says the door was bolted from inside and the transom open only a slit." He pushed a thumb toward Lydia. "She unscrewed some gadget to get the transom open and climbed through to unbolt the door."

Nicholson looked at Lydia. She said, "I was the only one with small enough hands to get a screwdriver through the crack."

Nicholson looked back at his partner. "The guy left by the fire escape?"

"There isn't any," Carter informed him.

"Hmm. Then he must have still been there when they found the body. Maybe hiding in the bathroom. He must have sneaked out when they left the room to call us."

Carter shook his head. "Simms says they had the same thought, and checked both the bathroom and closet." He looked at Weygand. "That right, mister?"

Weygand nodded. "I even looked under the bed."

"You mean we got a locked room mystery?" Nicholson asked in a querulous voice.

"Nope," Carter said. "It just narrows down to only one possible means of exit. There's a foot-wide ledge that runs clear around the building just below the window. A guy who didn't get dizzy could work his way along it to another room."

"Who's in the rooms either side of Hartman's?" Nicholson asked.

Simms said, "They're both vacant."

"I looked at them," Carter said. "The windows of both are closed, but unlocked. The guy could have pushed either up, then closed it again after he was inside. The doors have spring locks, so once he stepped out in the hall and pulled the door closed behind him, there'd be no sign of anybody ever being in the room."

Nicholson asked, "What's the doc say?"

"Dead three to five hours, which would make it

three-thirty to five-thirty this afternoon. Probably closer to five-thirty."

"How do you figure that?"

"Simms delivered the guy a pint of bourbon at noon, a second one at two-thirty. If it took him two and a half hours to kill the first, it probably took at ieast as long to kill the second, which would take him to five o'clock. And both are empty."

Nicholson nodded. "That's logical. Where do we go from here?"

"You can call the ice wagon and the fingerprint boys and stand by here to show them around. Have the fingerprint guys catch the windows in the rooms both sides of 714 too. I'll take these people down to headquarters to get their stories."

Jules Weygand stood up. "I'd better move my car then, Sergeant. It's parked in the hotel loading zone."

Simms said, "I'll move it for you, Mr. Weygand, and you can pick up the keys at the desk when you come back. I'll put it on the hotel lot."

Weygand handed over the keys and Simms said, "I'll put Mrs. Hartman's bag in her room too. It's 521, Mrs. Hartman."

"Thank you," Lydia said.

"Okay, folks," Sergeant Carter said. "Let's take a ride over to headquarters."

Police headquarters was only two blocks away, also on lower Pearl Street. Sergeant Carter ushered them into an elevator, and when they got off upstairs, led them to a door lettered: HOMICIDE AND ARSON. Beyond the door was a large squadroom with several desks in it. The only person in the room was a man in shirtsleeves talking on a phone at one of the desks. Carter seated himself behind another desk on the opposite side of the room and waved Lydia and Weygand to a pair of nearby chairs.

"Smoke?" he asked, extending a pack of cigarettes.

Both Weygand and Lydia shook their heads. Carter lit one for himself, leaned back in his chair and regarded Lydia from beneath his drooping lids.

"I understand the dead man was your husband, Mrs. Hartman. That right?"

Lydia nodded.

"And you're here from Rochester?"

"That's right. Jules here too."

"Uh-huh. What was your husband doing here?"

"Just getting drunk," she said, flushing slightly. "He's been doing that recently. But up until this time he's always holed up in some Rochester hotel."

"This is just something recent? His drinking, I mean."

"The last few weeks. He's been depressed over business matters."

"Oh? What was his business?"

"Jim and Jules, here, were partners in the Weygand and Hartman Realty Company. They filed for bankruptcy three weeks ago and the company is in receivership. It was all Jim's fault, really."

"How's that?" Carter asked.

"He—he misappropriated some funds. Jules found it out too late to save the business. He's been wonderful about it. He could have had Jim prosecuted and imprisoned."

"That wouldn't have saved anything," Weygand said dryly. "It would just have sent Jim to jail."

Carter turned his attention to Weygand. "Weren't you a little sore at your partner?"

"That's an understatement," Weygand said in the same dry tone. "I *would* have sent him to jail if it weren't for Lydia. I didn't want to hurt her."

"Oh? Why so considerate?"

"She hadn't done anything," Weygand said reasonably. "And I happen to like her."

After studying him for a moment, Carter turned back to Lydia. "How'd you know your husband was here in Buffalo?"

"Jules phoned me about five P.M. I had asked him to keep an eye on my husband, because Jim's been so depressed, I feared he might do something desperate. When Jules said my husband had registered here at the Redmill Hotel, and was having whisky delivered to his room, I took the six P.M. train here. I got in at seven-thirty and Jules met me at the train."

"Hmm. If you were in Rochester at five P.M., I guess you're cleared as a suspect." He swung his gaze back to Weygand. "You verify her story?"

"Of course," Weygand said in surprise. "You didn't actually suspect her of doing this thing, did you?"

"The wife is always a routine suspect when a man's murdered. Now about you. You tailed him here from Rochester, huh?"

"Not exactly. I watched him buy a bus ticket to Buffalo, drove here and picked him up at the bus depot again. When he checked in at the Redmill, I arranged with the desk clerk to let me know if he had any orders sent to his room. When I learned he was having whisky delivered, I phoned Lydia."

"I see. Seems to me you went to an awful lot of trouble for a guy who'd made you bankrupt."

Weygand flushed. "I wasn't doing it for him. It was a favor for Lydia."

"Kind of fond of her, huh?"

Weygand's flush deepened. "What are you getting at, Sergeant?"

"I'll spell it out for you," Carter said. "Hartman's

wallet was in his hip pocket with sixty-three dollars in it, so the motive wasn't robbery. He was a stranger here, so it isn't likely he had any local enemies. You admit you had a grudge against him and you're fond of his wife. You married, Mr. Weygand?"

After staring at him for a time, Weygand said hotly, "No. But if you're accusing me—"

"I'm not accusing anybody, just yet," the sergeant interrupted. "I'm just pointing out that you seem to have a couple of good motives, and you tailed him here all the way from Rochester."

"But that was at my request," Lydia protested, her face paling. "I was afraid Jim might try to kill himself."

"Maybe your boy friend was afraid he wouldn't," Carter said cynically. "Until we turn up a better suspect, guess we'll have to hold you a while for investigation, Weygand."

Jules Weygand puffed up with indignation. But before he could open his mouth, the squadroom door opened and Harry Nicholson walked in. He was carrying a small paper bag in his hand.

As Nicholson approached the desk, Sergeant Carter said, "Get anything?"

"The lab boys are still lifting prints. The guys from the morgue have been and gone." He set the paper bag on the desk. "You can handle this. It's already been checked for prints, and there aren't any."

Sergeant Carter peered into the bag, then reached in and drew out an open, thin-bladed clasp knife with a blade about five inches long. The blade was darkly stained.

Laying it on his desk blotter, Carter asked, "Anyone recognize this?"

Lydia managed to overcome her revulsion at the dark stain and leaned forward to examine the knife more closely. In its tan-colored bone handle the initials "J.H." were inset in silver.

"It's my husband's," she said in a whisper. "He always carried it."

Carter looked up at Nicholson. "So he was killed with his own knife, huh? Probably he was passed out on the bed when the killer entered his room."

"What I figured," Nicholson said. "Of course we'll have to get the lab to run a check of the blood type on the knife against Hartman's, but I'll bet a beer they match."

"No bet," Carter said. "Where'd you turn it up?"

"I was making a routine check of Weygand's car," Nicholson said casually. "It was in the glove compartment."

It was nearly midnight when Lydia got back to her hotel room. She had stood by to protest Jules' innocence to the two unbelieving homicide officers, then had phoned a lawyer, waited until he arrived, and had outlined the whole situation to him. None of it had done any good. There was no bail in first-degree homicide cases, so Jules Weygand was in jail.

Her performance had helped her own case, she knew, even if it hadn't helped Jules's. It would have been inconvenient if the police had suspected collusion between her and Jules, even though there had been none. As it was, they had seemed rather admiring that she had stood by her husband in his trouble to the extent that she had sent a friend to watch over him in case Jules attempted suicide.

Of course nobody, including Jules, suspected the

real reason for her worry over Jim was that he might commit suicide before she could arrange a suitable accident.

Slipping off her dress and slip, she hung them neatly in the closet. As she peeled off her left stocking, she frowned at the small bloodstain on the inside of her thigh. Then she saw that a run had started where the point of the knife had punctured the nylon when she thrust it down inside the stocking.

Before removing the other stocking, she went into the bathroom and washed away the tiny blood-stain. Reaching down into the other stocking, she drew out a folded slip of paper, opened it and read it for the first time. There hadn't been time to read it in Jim's room, of course; only time to get it out of sight.

The note was almost illegible, obviously written in the last stages of drunkenness. But amid the erratic scrawling she could make out the phrase: "Sorry I have to take this way out, Lydia, but—" Nothing more was decipherable, but that was enough to indicate it was a suicide note.

Tearing it into small pieces, she flushed it away.

It was a good thing she worked for the insurance company where Jim was insured, she thought. Otherwise, she might have been unaware that his fifty-thousand-dollar policy contained a suicide clause which voided it in the event he took his own life.

It was only right that she should salvage something from a marriage to which she had devoted ten years, Lydia thought. And if she hadn't removed the knife from Jim's chest and the note from his hand, she would have nothing to show for the ten years.

TRICK

by Gil Brewer

Chauncey wrinkled his thin, leathery face in a sneer.
Virginia was so stupid and slow.

"You got the envelope ready?" he asked.

"Yes, darling."

"Cut the comedy. What's with this 'darling' bit?"

"I thought you liked it."

"Step over here, and I'll show you how much I like
it."

"You just want to hit me again," Virginia said.

Chauncey laughed. It was loud, bold, and it was directed at the girl. "You need hitting. A guy said a wife
should be struck every so often, just like a Chinese
gong."

"I'm not your wife."

They looked at each other across the one-room
apartment. Virginia's blond hair was ratty, hanging
straight to her shoulders. She was thin, her bones were
tired-looking knots, and the skimpy blue minidress
didn't help. Blue eyes peered from deep sockets with a
curious sadness. Her mouth was small, red and tight.
Below high cheekbones, the cheeks were sunken, and
deep lines grooved from each nostril to the corners of
her lips.

She said, "Why can't I leave, Chauncey? Why d'you
hang onto me? Why won't you let me go?" Her voice

was a trying whine, touched with resignation.

" 'Cause I like you around, baby."

That's all he ever told her, but she knew, and he knew she knew, that she was his beating post. It made him grin inside. He needed her. He needed someone to subjugate, and the girl was perfect. They traveled everywhere together, and he kept her in a perpetual state of suspense. She knew she would be bounced around, but when? It always happened sooner than she expected.

A short con artist, Chauncey had come over from London and found good pickings in the cities along the Eastern seaboard. He liked having Virginia with him. They lived in cheap hotel rooms, an occasional dusty, linoleum-floored apartment.

"Where's the envelope?" Chauncey asked. "I told you to fix it."

"In your breast pocket. It's all addressed."

"The gimmick?"

"In your side pocket. It's cut just right, and I found a sheet of green. You shouldn't take those chances. I keep telling you to use a one-dollar bill, Chauncey. You only lose a dollar, and it's safer that way."

"Why give 'em a buck?"

"Anyway, everything's ready. You picked a spot?"

"Yeah. Stan's Liquors, on Second Avenue. Plenty business, but lots of dead time just the same. And Stan's a plowhead."

"You taking a gun?"

"You know it."

"Why d'you take a gun, Chauncey? It's such a chance. Suppose something happened? Suppose you used it? What then?"

"Shut your yap. You make me sick."

"Chauncey. Let me go home. I'm sick of all this.

Traipsing from one town to another. You always beating up on me."

He leaped across the room. She cringed, plastering herself against the flowered wallpaper. He grabbed her by the shoulders and shook her. He was laughing quietly. He shook her hard. Then he slapped her face viciously. He gave her a push and she sprawled across the bed, the springs jouncing.

"Please, Chauncey," she whined.

"Please, please, please. That's all you can say. You're stupid. I carry you, don't I? Well? Then be thankful."

"But—why? Why d'you want me around?"

He sneered, rocking on his heels. "Because I like you around, see? Ain't that enough?" He was dressed nattily in pale gray, and a maroon tie with a tiny diamond stickpin. He reached to the foot of the bed, snagged a soft felt hat. "Where's the change?"

"Right on the table. Nineteen dollars."

Chauncey pocketed the pile of crumpled bills, the extra loose change. He touched his breast pocket, fingered his side jacket pocket. Virginia watched him with her lips open.

"C'mon. We'll go take 'im."

"Do I have to come?"

"You know you have to come. You're my good luck piece." He laughed. "A hot one, ain't it? Get it? On your feet, stupid. Chauncey Moorehouse rides again."

"A lousy twenty dollars," Virginia said.

"It's enough. Tomorrow I'm gonna work five twenties. I'm gonna do it every day for a week. We spend the rest of this afternoon lining up joints."

"Okay. I'm ready."

They left the Hobart Arms, strolled along the street. Every now and again Chauncey yanked at Virginia's arm, and she would yank back and glare at him. Then maybe he would knuckle her in the kidney. On the corner, he tapped the gun holstered under his left arm. It felt comfortable. He'd never used it, but it made him feel big time, somehow.

"I'm not coming in," Virginia said.

"Who asked you? Don't come in, then."

"I wish we could have a bottle."

"Bottle help you, baby?"

"Some gin, maybe? Something?"

"See what I can do."

She was immediately excited. "Would you Chauncey?"

"I'll see."

He gave it some thought. Four bucks, probably, for a fifth. Not for stupid, either. He could use it; he felt like a drunk. It was just what he needed. Well, wait and see.

"Here we are. Stan's Liquors."

"There's nobody inside."

"Yeah. Okay, you wait."

"I'll be right here, Chauncey."

"You better be, stupid."

"Don't say that."

"Ah, shut up."

He left her, walked to the entrance, and stepped inside. It was a small closet-like store, with bottles in the windows, bottles racked by the door, bottles on the walls, on the counter, everywhere. Hand-lettered signs proclaimed vast reductions in prices.

"Hi, there," Chauncey said to the plump, pale-faced man behind the counter by the cash register. The man wore a tan shirt, open at the throat, and black trousers. He had an open, almost merry face.

"Fine," the man said. "What can I do you for?"

Chauncey smiled pleasantly, stepped quickly to the counter. "In a darned rush," he said. "Got to meet my girl." He began hauling out the mass of crumpled bills, the loose change. "Could you give me a twenty for this change, here? What my girl don't know won't hurt her."

"Sure, sure." The pale-faced counterman punched the cash register, withdrew a twenty, snapped it, and handed it to Chauncey.

"Thanks," Chauncey said. "Mailing it to my brother. He's in a fix in Tucson, tight up. I can only spare twenty, the way things are." As he talked, he drew out the stamped, addressed envelope—phony name and address—and somehow the twenty dollar bill vanished and the slip of paper, dark green, was in his palm, and then inside the envelope. He sealed the envelope slowly, tapped it against his fingers as the counterman finished counting the change. "Thanks, again," Chauncey said. "Where's the nearest—"

"There's only nineteen bucks here. You're short a dollar."

"What?"

"Right." The pale-faced man shook his head. "Sorry, old buddy. But that's how it is. Here, you count it."

"No. I believe you. Now, ain't that a hot one?" Chauncey shook his head and gusted a sigh. "You're positive?"

The counterman nodded. "Yup."

Chauncey's face lit up. "I got it," he said. "Here. You just hold this twenty, in the envelope. Rather than break it open and all, I'll run down an' meet my girl, get the buck from her. Be right back. Okay?" Chauncey shoveled the nineteen dollars from the counter back into his pocket.

The counterman was hesitant. He didn't want Chaun-

cey to think he didn't trust him. Sighing, he took the envelope. "Hurry it up, though. I'm closing in ten minutes."

"Thanks," Chauncey said. "I'll make it snappy."

He started for the door. The counterman was placing
the envelope on the cash register. Chauncey felt good.
He'd made twenty dollars. The world was right.

The counterman's back was turned. Chauncey paused
by a liquor rack, grinned to himself, lifted a bottle,
tucked it under his arm and headed for the bright sunlight.

"Wait!" It was the counterman. He'd seen him.

Chauncey whirled. Somebody was coming in the
door, a short, fat man in black. The counterman's face
was a dark cloud. Chauncey was caught with the goods,
and it was a lousy feeling.

Then he knew he couldn't wait, couldn't do any
false apologizing, because if the counterman ever
opened that envelope it would be a mess.

"The hell with you," Chauncey said, turning for the
door. The short man in black was in the way.

"Stand still or I'll shoot," the counterman said.

Chauncey turned again. The counterman was nervously holding a revolver.

Chauncey acted on impulse. He dropped the bottle
and it broke. He cursed, grabbed the .32 automatic
from its holster under his left arm, and pumped four
slugs into the counterman. It was over with so quickly,
Chauncey couldn't really believe it had happened.
The plump man sank behind his counter, making
strange noises, bleeding in the chest.

The short man in black threw up his arms as
Chauncey headed for the door. They collided. Chauncey cursed, brandished the automatic. The man scur-

ried for the side of the liquor store. Chauncey made the street.

"Virginia!" he called.

She wasn't there, and he couldn't wait. He ran for the corner, thinking, *Now I've done it, now I've done it.* He reached the corner, saw a cab, flagged it, and was inside in seconds. He kept stretching, looking for Virginia, but there was no sign of her.

He left the cab a block from the apartment house and hurried to the apartment. Virginia must have got tired of waiting and headed for home.

She wasn't there. The apartment was empty, and the more he glanced around, the emptier it looked.

He'd made it. He'd got the twenty—and he had killed a man. But nobody knew him in town. They'd only been here two days, and the only person who'd seen him was the short, fat man dressed in black. He'd made a clean getaway. He began to breathe easier.

Then he checked the apartment, and realized Virginia's suitcase was gone. He got tight all over, because he knew she'd finally done it. She'd taken the chance and scrammed. She was gone, and he was alone again. That was that.

Well, what loss? Not much. He could find another. After over a year of making her go with him, knocking her around, ridiculing her, destroying her, he dismissed her from his mind.

He grinned and took out the twenty, and looked at it. He had over a hundred dollars. It would take him to another town, and he would leave immediately. He began packing.

There was a knock at the door.

He stood there. Now, who the hell would that be? It couldn't be trouble, anyway.

Then he knew. It was Virginia. She'd come back. She needed him.

He hurried to the door, swung it open, and started yelling something at her. He closed his mouth.

The uniformed cop stepped quickly aside. The short, fat man in black shouted, "That's him!"

A plainclothes cop stepped forward. "Chauncey Moorehouse?"

"Yeah—yes."

"I'm arresting you for the murder of Stanley Griner, owner of Stan's Liquor Store, on Second Avenue. Mr. Moorehouse, anything you say now may be held as evidence."

Chauncey stared at him.

The cop had a big red face with small brown eyes. He looked very grim. He leaned forward, rapped Chauncey under the arm, plucked the automatic from its holster, and stood there staring at it. He sniffed it.

"Ballistics will confirm it, anyway," he said.

"But," Chauncey said, "how—?"

"Oh, yeah," the plainclothesman said. "Guess you would like to know." He drew an envelope from his pocket. "See?" he said. "Right here. Mr. Griner lived long enough to say you'd left this behind."

"But, that ain't no—"

The cop was grim. "It's not just the envelope, Mr. Moorehouse. It's what's inside."

The cop drew out the slip of dark green paper, and showed it to Chauncey:

Chauncey Moorehouse did this. Address Apt. 2C, Hobart Arms, Sixteenth and 3rd Avenue.

It was in Virginia's flowery handwriting.

OLDER THAN SPRINGTIME

by Syd Hoff

Mr. Metcalf couldn't stand anything old. "Let's redo the whole house," he said.

He said it every year.

"Julian!" His wife tried to reason with him. "Let's keep the bed at least, the new floor lamps, the coffee table, that oil painting over the fireplace . . ."

No, everything had to go. She knew better than to argue with him.

Even at the office: "Langley, get rid of the girls," he told his assistant manager regularly. "Hire new ones, younger ones."

"But, Mr. Metcalf, we hired these girls ten months ago. They're just getting the hang of things."

"I don't care, Langley. They look old, they *are* old. All they do is take up collections for each other when they get married. Let only Miss Conover stay. The others, fire."

"Miss Conover?"

"Yes, the one with the dancing eyes." She was the symbol of youth to him, whether she was typing, filing, standing by the water fountain, or munching a cream cheese and jelly sandwich downstairs in the Busy Bee Cafeteria—blonde, frail, wispy.

It was a pleasure for Mr. Metcalf to come to the office every day, to look at Miss Conover without her knowing, to sit alongside her in the Busy Bee at lunchtime, instead of taking himself uptown to the Oak Room of the Plaza where business could be discussed, stimulated.

But who cared about business with Miss Conover so close? Even the counterman couldn't take his eyes off her. "Wanna 'nother cuppa coffee, Miss Conover? Wanna 'nother glassa water?"

"No, Mike, thanks."

Damn counterman, damn all those guys half his age. They couldn't possibly appreciate such a nice girl, such a nice *young* girl.

"Miss Conover, would you like the afternoon off?"

"Why, Mr. Metcalf!"

"I said, would you like the afternoon off?"

"But Mr. Metcalf, sir, I've got so much work to do, such an awful *lot* of work."

"Blast the work, Miss Conover! We can take a carriage through the park, look up at the leaves in the trees. It's spring, Miss Conover! Spring!"

They took the carriage. Mr. Metcalf didn't look up at the leaves. He only looked at Miss Conover. She was so young. *She* was spring!

"Thank you for a lovely day, Mr. Metcalf. You're a nice man."

His face fell.

"Did I say something wrong, sir?"

"You make me sound so old. Couldn't you possibly think of me as a nice *fellow?* As Julian?"

She laughed, kept laughing as she raced up the steps, turned to wave a garland of flowers at him getting back in the cab.

Home. Mr. Metcalf grimaced as he paid the driver. The whole facade needed sandblasting. Or had they just done that last year, and the year before?

Valerie greeted him at the door. "Like it?" she asked, grinning.

"Like what?"

"My skin. I had another one of those treatments to-day. The doctor thinks I look fifteen years younger."

You look like Whistler's mother, Mr. Metcalf wanted to say.

"I have a surprise for you, Julian." She led him into the library, to an old man.

"What's *he* doing here?"

"Julian!"

"I thought we had agreed to keep your father in a retirement home."

"We did, Julian. But they had a fire there today. I'll have to find him another place."

"You better find it fast!"

"I will, I will."

The maid appeared. Dinner was ready.

"I'll eat in my room," said Mr. Metcalf.

He ate upstairs the next night and the night after that, too. Just thinking of the old man made him al-most lose his appetite. His wife knew it, but there was nothing she could do. Retirement homes were a great business. They all had waiting lists a mile long.

One night Mr. Metcalf threw his tray to the floor, went charging down the stairs. "I don't care if you have to give your father an overdose of sleeping pills, get rid of him!" he shouted.

"Julian, I won't have you talking that way in front of Papa."

"Aw, the old man's deaf. Look at him sitting there, staring. He can't hear a thing."

"I know, but it's—it's indecent."

"Indecent? What I'm suggesting would be a favor for him, an act of mercy. How old is he anyway? Ninety-five?"

"Eighty-five."

"Okay, eighty-five. Suppose we can't get him into another retirement home and you can't get adequate help. How would you like to go on taking care of him like this for the next ten years, feeding him, changing him?"

"Please try to understand, Julian. As long as I have a roof over my head, my father stays."

"And you try to understand, Valerie. If he stays I won't be able to go on living under that very same roof!" He ran out of the house, slamming the door behind him.

Valerie went to her father, knelt by his side. "Papa, Papa," she said, forcing a smile. "Here, finish your tea and toast. Open your mouth, Papa. Let me feed you . . ."

Her husband didn't take a cab. He walked across town to Miss Conover's, rang her bell, kept on ringing and ringing. He just wanted to bury his head in her lap and cry, cry like a little boy.

No one answered. Mr. Metcalf walked the streets aimlessly, then went home. The whole house was asleep.

He went into his father-in-law's room. Was the old man only sleeping? Sometimes it was difficult to tell with old people, very difficult.

Mr. Metcalf got the sleeping pills, mixed them in a glass of water, held the concoction to the old man's lips. "Here, Papa, drink."

The toothless mouth sucked at the glass, went on sucking.

Mr. Metcalf undressed and got into bed without awakening his wife, snuggled close to her. The poor dear, the poor old dear. She'd need him now, could have him for a little while anyway.

He left the house early the next morning, so as to be at the office when Miss Conover arrived.

"Good morning, sir." . . . "May I help you, sir?" . . . "Is there anyone in particular you wished to see, sir?"

Damn new girls. They didn't know him.

Ten o'clock . . . eleven o'clock . . . eleven forty-five . . . Mr. Metcalf didn't even feel like looking at the mail on his desk.

"Hey, Langley, you didn't let Miss Conover go, too, did you?"

"Oh, no, sir. But wasn't she the one they were taking up a collection for yesterday, the one who got engaged?"

Mr. Metcalf rushed downstairs to the Busy Bee. Miss Conover was behind the counter with Mike, younger looking than ever in an apron, with a pencil behind her ear.

"Did you get my letter of resignation, Mr. Metcalf? I left it on your desk. Mike here offered me a job with real security and I couldn't turn him down. Thanks for everything, sir—I mean—ha! ha!—Julian."

Mr. Metcalf went directly home. He heard his wife crying as he was putting away his hat and stick.

"It's Papa," Valerie said. "I didn't want to bother you at the office. He just didn't wake up this morning. They took him away a little while ago."

Mr. Metcalf was holding her close when the phone rang.

"It's the Eastern Star Retirement Home," said the maid. "They say they have an opening now."

"Tell them it's too late," sobbed Valerie.

"No, I'll tell them," said Mr. Metcalf.

Suddenly he didn't feel too young himself, felt even less young after he had finished talking and called the police.

DON'T SIT UNDER THE APPLE TREE

by Helen Nielsen

It was exactly ten minutes before three when Loren returned to her apartment. The foyer was empty—a glistening, white and black tile emptiness of Grecian simplicity which left no convenient nooks or alcoves where a late party-goer could linger with her escort in a prolonged embrace, or where the manager—in the unlikely event that he was concerned—could spy out the nocturnal habits of his tenants. Loren moved swiftly across the foyer, punctuating its silence with the sharp tattoo of her heels on the tile and the soft rustling of her black taffeta evening coat. Black for darkness; black for stealth. She stepped into the automatic elevator and pressed the button for the seventeenth floor. The door closed and the elevator began its silent climb. Only then did she breathe a bit easier, reassuring herself that she was almost safe.

There was an apex of terror, a crisis at which everything and every place became a pulsing threat. Loren wore her terror well. A watcher—had there been an invisible watcher in the elevator—would not have been aware of it. He would have seen only a magnetically attractive woman—mature, poised, a faint dusting of premature gray feathering her almost black hair. The trace of tension in her face and eyes would have been attributed to fatigue. The slight impatience which prompted her repeated glances at the floor indicator above the doors would have passed for a natural desire to get home and put an end to an over-long, wearisome day.

In a sense, the watcher would have been right.

The elevator doors opened at the seventeenth floor, and Loren stepped out into a carpeted corridor of emptiness. Pausing only to verify the emptiness, she hurried to the door of her apartment. The key was in her gloved hand before she reached it. She let herself in, closed the door behind her, and leaned against it until she could hear the latch click. For a moment her body sagged and clung to the door as if nailed there, and then she pulled herself upright.

Above the lamp on the hall table—the light turned softly, as she had left it—a sunburst clock splashed against the wall in glittering elegance. The time was eight minutes before three. There was work to be done. Loren switched off the lamp. The long room ahead became an arrangement of grays and off-blacks set against the slightly paler bank of fully draped windows at the end of it; but halfway between the hall and the windows, a narrow rectangle of light cut a pattern across the grays. The light came from the bedroom. Loren moved toward it, catching, as she did so, the sound of a carefully modulated feminine voice dictating letters.

To Axel Torberg and Sons,

Kungsgaten 47,
Stockholm, Sweden.

Gentlemen.

In regard to your inquiry of February 11, last:

I am sorry to inform you that full payment for your last shipment cannot be made until the damaged merchandise (see our correspondence of Jan. 5) has been replaced.

Having done satisfactory business with your firm for the past twenty years, we feel confident that you will maintain this good will by taking immediate action.

Very Truly Yours,
Loren Banion
Vice President
John O. Banion, Inc.

Loren entered the bedroom. The voice came again, now in a warmer and more informal tone.

Katy, get this off airmail the first thing in the morning. Poor old Axel's getting forgetful in his dotage and has to be prodded. Okay, Doll—?
Next letter:

To Signor Luigi Manfredi,
    Via Proconsolo,
    Florence . . . .

The room was heavily carpeted. Loren made no sound as she crossed quickly to the French windows, barely glancing at the dictograph which stood on the bedside work table. It was still partly open. The night wind worried the edge of the soft drapes which gave concealment as Loren, pulling them aside only a finger width, peered out at the scene below. The seventeenth floor was one floor higher than the recreation deck. The pool lights were out; but there was a moon, and young Cherry Morgan's shapely legs were clearly visible

stretched out from the sheltering canvas sides of one of
the swinging lounges. There were legs other than Cherry's—trousered legs; identity unknown. With her par-
ents abroad, Cherry was playing the field.

> . . . if you will wire this office on the date of ship-
> ment, we will have our representative at the docks
> to make inspection on arrival. . . .

The voice of Loren Banion continued to dictate behind her. Loren listened and slowly relaxed. She
had, she now realized, been gripping at the draperies
until her fingers were aching. She released the cloth
and walked back to the bed—no longer swiftly, but
with a great weariness as if she had come a very
long distance, running all the way. She sank down
slowly and sat on the edge of the bed. The dictograph
was now a droning nuisance, but a necessary one.
Cherry Morgan could hear it, and that was important.

".' . . Honestly, Mrs. Banion, I don't know how you
can work as late as you do! Sometimes I hear you up
there dictating all night long."

"Not all night, Cherry. I never work past three. Doctor's orders."

"Doctor's orders? What a drag! I'm glad I don't
have your doctor. If I'm going to work until three in
the morning it's got to be at something more interesting
than business correspondence!"

And the fact that Cherry Morgan frequently worked
past three was the reason the dictograph continued to
play.

> . . . Very Truly Yours,
> Oh, you know the rest, Katy. On second

thought, give the sign off more flourish. Signor Manfredi probably sings Don Jose in his shower.

A small crystal clock stood beside the dictating machine. Loren glanced at it; it was six minutes before three. She had done well. A year of catching planes, meeting trains and keeping spot appointments, had paid off in timing. It was all over, and she was safe. The tension could ebb away now, and the heaviness lift; and yet, it was all she could do to raise up the small black evening bag she had been clutching in her left hand, open it, and withdraw the gun. She held the gun cupped in the palm of her right hand. She looked about the room for some place to hide it; then, unable to look at it any longer, jammed it back into the bag and tossed it on the table beside the clock. The time—five minutes before three. It was close enough. She got up and switched off the machine. Then she removed her gloves, shoes, coat, and went into the bathroom. She left the door open—the shower could be heard for some distance at this hour—and returned exactly five minutes later wearing a filmy gown and negligee. She got into bed and switched off the light; but now her eyes were caught by a glittering object that would not let them go. It was such a frivolous telephone—French styling sprayed with gold. It was magnetic and compelling. It seemed almost a living thing; and a living thing could be denounced.

"Not tonight," Loren said. "You won't ring tonight."

It had all started with a telephone call—long distance, Cairo to New York City.

"Mr. Banion calling Miss Loren Donell . . . thank you. Here's your party, Mr. Banion."

And then John's voice, annihilating miles.

"Loren—? Hold on tight. I've got one question: will you marry me?"

It could have happened only that way. John wasted neither time nor words. She had clung to the telephone, suddenly feeling quite schoolgirlish and dizzy.

"But, John, what about Celeste?"

"What about her? She's flipped over a Spanish bull-fighter, and he's expensive. We've finally struck a deal. She's in Paris now getting a divorce."

"I can't believe it!"

"Neither can I, but it's true. I thought I'd never get rid of that—of my dear wife, Celeste." And then John's voice had become very serious. "You know what it's been like for me these past years, Loren. Celeste trapped me—I admit that. She wanted status and money, and she got both. I got—well, now I'm getting free and I suppose I should just be grateful for the education. Loren, I don't say these things well—but I love you."

At that moment, the telephone had been a lifeline pulling Loren out of the quicksand of loneliness. She clung to it until John's voice blasted her silence.

"Well! I want an answer! Will you marry me?"

Laughing and crying, she had answered, "Yes, yes, yes, yes—"

"Hold it!" John ordered. "While you're talking, I can be flying. See you tomorrow."

Tomorrow . . .

Rain at Kennedy—hard, slanting, and completely unnoticed as John bounded off the plane like a school-boy. There was much to be done before the cable from Paris announced the divorce had been granted, and one of the many things concerned a change in office procedure. Loren discovered it one morning when she found her old office cleaned out, and, investigating, a new name on the door of the office next to John's.

LOREN BANION
VICE-PRESIDENT

"Only a little premature," he explained. "You might as well get used to the name."

"It's not the name—it's the title!" Loren exclaimed.

"Why not the title? You've been doing the job for years; I've only belatedly given you the status. Belatedly," he repeated, "this, too." It was then that he gave her the ring, almost shyly. "Oh, Loren why does it take so long to learn to distinguish the real from the phony? You are real, aren't you, Loren? You're not one of those scheming females."

"Oh, but I am," Loren insisted. "I've been deliberately getting under your nose for years."

John had laughed. Under his nose meant only one thing at the moment. He kissed her, quickly.

"That I like. That I'll buy any day. That's not what I meant. I meant that you're not one of the phonies—the honky-tonk phonies. All out front and nothing to live with. I want to grow old with you, Loren. You're the only—" He hesitated, groping for a word. "—the only pure woman I've ever known."

It was terrible how grave John's face had become, Loren drew away.

"Please—no pedestals," she protested. "It's so cold up there!"

"It's not cold here!"

He had taken her in his arms, then, and he was right. It was warm; it was a place to rest at last. But then his arms tightened, and his fingers dug into her arms

until she wanted to cry out. It was the first shadow of
fear to come.

"You're real," he said. "You have to be real. I
couldn't stand being fooled again!"

"I couldn't stand being fooled again!"

Loren stared at the telephone on the table. It was silent; but John's words were ringing in her mind. She
glanced at the clock. Sleep was impossible, but nothing could be unusual tonight, and within ten minutes
after Loren Banion concluded her dictation, she always turned off the lamp. The darkness came—complete at first, and then a finger of moonlight from the
open window probed across the carpet. Below, the silver sound of a girl's laughter was quickly muffled
in sudden remembrance of the hour.

The hour. The hour was only ten minutes spent.
The long hour before four . . .

The honeymoon had been in Miami and off-Miami
waters. John was a fisherman—unsuccessful but incor-
rigible. Monday, Tuesday, Wednesday without a catch.
It was no wonder Sam McGregor, an Atlanta account
they had discovered vacationing at their hotel, had insisted on an hour of solace at the Flotsam and Jetsam on
the beach. It was a shanty-type bar—one of the higher
bracket shanties—where the drinks were long and the
shadows cool. Loren was too happy to see details in
the Grotto-like shadows; but someone had seen clearly.
Very clearly. It was an informal place for customers in
shorts and bathing suits, and the only entertainment
rippled from the busy fingers of a pianist in T shirt
and dungarees who wheeled his diminutive instrument from booth to booth. He wasn't meant to be heard
or noticed, and only rarely tipped; and Loren wasn't
really aware of him at all until, above John's and Sam's

ribbing laughter, a tinkling sound became a melody.
She looked up. The small piano was no more than three
feet away, and behind it sat a man she had never expected to see again.

"Don't sit under the apple tree with anyone else but
me . . ."

He played not too well; but he did enjoy his work.
His smile seemed to indicate that he enjoyed it very
much. His smile . . .

"Loren—are you all right?"

John's voice brought Loren back from the far away
place Loren's mind had gone reeling.

"You look shook up, honey. Don't tell me that you
got seasick today. Honestly, Sam, this woman can take
more punishment . . ."

When John's voice stopped, he couldn't have known
too much then. That was impossible. But he seemed to
sense that the piano player had something to do with
Loren being disturbed. He pulled a bill out of his pocket
and placed it on top of the piano.

"How about hoisting anchor, sailor?" he said. "I'm
afraid we're not very musical in this booth."

The piano player's smile broadened and one hand
closed over the bill. "Anything you say, Mr. Banion.
I only thought it would be nice to salute the newlyweds."

"You know me?" John asked.

"Why, everybody knows you, Mr. Banion. Didn't you
see your picture in the paper the day you flew down?
Nice catch, Mr. Banion." And then, with another smile
for Loren. "Nice catch, Mrs. Banion. A very nice
catch."

The piano rolled on, picking up something with a
calypso beat. The incident had taken only a moment,
but having sensed that something was amiss, Sam had
said brightly—

"Enterprising chap. They don't miss a trick down here. How about another round?"

Loren stood up. "You two—yes," she said. "No more for me. I'm going back to the hotel."

"Loren—why? What's wrong?"

John must not ask that question; he must not look that concerned. She laughed her gayest and confessed—

"I'm afraid you'll have to stop bragging about me, John. I did get sea-sick this afternoon, and now I'm almost hung on one drink. No—not hung enough for you to break this up. You stay on with Sam. I'm going to get some air."

Air, wind, and a long walk along the beach—nothing erased Ted Lockard. He should be dead. Men died in a war. They stopped answering letters, and they never came back. One assumed they had died. But not Ted. Ted was alive, and his smooth voice, so thrilling to a girl, had an oily quality maturity could identify. There were men who lived off their charms, even as did some women.

"A nice catch, Mrs. Banion. A very nice catch."

Loren wasn't intoxicated, but she was sick. A girl had written wild, foolish letters, and Ted Lockard probably kept all of his love letters the way some men kept hunting trophies—or securities. He would try to reach her some way—she knew that. And she was vulnerable; not because of a youthful human failure, but because of John's conception of her. She had to be perfect in order to compensate his pride, for having been so deceived by Celeste.

Luck was with her. That night, a wire from Mexico City sending John south. Loren returned to New York. But it was only a reprieve.

Celeste returned from Europe just before Christmas,

sans bullfighter and sans cash. There were telephone calls and wires, all ignored, and then, one day Celeste came to the office. John saw her. Loren wasn't aware of the meeting until it was over. John had asked her to go down to the docks and see Signor Manfredi's shipment through customs. The Signor's shipping department had only a vague idea of the transoceanic hazards for breakable materials. It was a task usually delegated to an employee of lesser status; but Loren thought nothing of it until she returned in time to pass Celeste in the outer office.

Celeste was icily majestic.

"Congratulations, Mrs. Banion," she said. "John looks in the pink. You always were a good manager."

Not too much—just enough. Celeste could make a prayer sound insulting.

Inside, Loren found John not at all in the pink. He was remote and grave.

"What was Celeste doing here?" she demanded.

"She came to wish us a Merry Christmas," John said bitterly.

Loren glanced down. John's checkbook was still on his desk.

"John—you gave her money!"

He didn't answer.

"Why? Hasn't she cost you enough? You don't owe her a thing!"

"Loyalty," John said.

His voice was strange.

"What?" Loren demanded.

"It's a word," John explained. "Just a word."

Then, suddenly, he turned toward her and grasped her shoulders with both hands, holding so tightly that she remembered what had happened the day he gave her the ring. For just an instant, she was actually afraid; and then he smiled sadly and let her go.

"Forget Celeste," he said. "It's a holiday season. I felt charitable."

Loren didn't. She left John abruptly and hurried back to the front office. Celeste was nowhere in sight. Katy sat at her desk, typing letters. She looked up as Loren spoke—

"Mrs. Ban—" she began, and then corrected herself. "The former Mrs. Banion—where did she go?"

"Out," Katy said.

Katy, sweet, wholesome, naive. What did she expect to learn from Katy? She strode across the reception room and entered the hall, arriving just in time to glimpse Celeste as she was being assisted into the elevator by an attentive man. They turned and faced her, and just before the doors closed Loren got a frontal view of Celeste's new adornment. Ted looked very handsome, and he smiled.

Merry Christmas, Loren. Merry Christmas and a Happy New Year. Santa had come early. It was the beginning of a long wait, of not knowing what Ted might have told Celeste, or what Celeste might have told John, or when Ted would make his move. John said nothing. Her own tension was the only change between them. After a time, she began to think she was suffering from nothing but the ancient feminine penchant for borrowing guilt.

Then, in the middle of January, John took the night plane to Cleveland.

"You could leave in the morning and still make that meeting in time," Loren protested.

John was adamant.

"I like to fly at night. It's smoother and I sleep all the way."

"Then I'll work on the correspondence."

"You work too hard, Loren. Why don't you let Katy do that?"

"John—please. I know these people. I've been handling your correspondence with them since dear Katy was taking her first typing lessons and getting used to having teeth without braces. Don't you know that I'm jealous of my work?"

"I should know," John said. "I'm jealous, too—of you. But I don't have to worry, do I?" His fingers stroked her cheek lightly. "No, I don't have to worry —not about Loren."

Loren, who lived on a pedestal where the life expectancy was so short.

She had worked that night until almost three, showered, and gone to bed. Sleep came immediately after work. She had to fight her way out of it when the telephone rang. Groping for the instrument, she noticed the illuminated face of the clock. It was exactly four. Nobody ever called anyone at four o'clock in the morning unless something terrible had happened.

"John—?"

She waited, suddenly fully awake and afraid. There was no answer. And then it began, so brightly, so spritely—one full chorus of a piano rendition of an old wartime melody:

"Don't Sit Under The Apple Tree With Anyone Else But Me . . ."

That was all.

The clock had always been silent. There was no reason for it to tick so loudly now. Loren stirred restlessly against the pillows and turned her head toward the source of her torment. Sleep was impossible. She pulled herself up higher against the pillows. Aside from the clock, there was no other sound. Silence from

the deck below. Cherry had closed up shop for the
night. The moonlight brought objects on the table out
of darkness. Loren's fingers found a cigarette, lighted
it, and then she sat back smoking and remembering . . .

She never told John about the four o'clock call. It
was Ted's signature, obviously; but what did he have in
mind? For days and nights after that call she waited
for his next move. Nothing happened. John returned
from Cleveland to find her thinner and tense.

"Working too hard," he scolded. "Loren, I won't al-
low this to go on! Katy's going to take on at least a
small part of your work."

She wanted to tell him about the call; but she couldn't
tell a part without revealing the whole.

*"Then reveal the whole, Loren. John is a sane, adult
human being. He'll laugh about it and send Ted packing."*

"Do you remember the McGregors?" John asked
suddenly. "Miami—our honeymoon?"

Loren remembered. Her mind had just been in the
same vicinity.

"I met Sam in Cleveland. He's broken—literally broken. His wife has gone to Reno, and Sam's shot. I've
seen that man fight his way through tight spots that
would have staggered Superman; but this has got him.
You women don't know what you can do to a man."

"Reno?" Loren echoed. "Why?"

John's face hardened. "The usual reason. Sam's a
busy man. Little time to play Casanova. They don't
have bullfighters in Atlanta; but they do have Casa-
novas. You would think a woman could tell the difference between love and flattery wouldn't you? But no, it
seems they all have the same weakness." And then the
bitterness ebbed out of John's voice. "Except one," he
added.

She told him nothing.

She continued to wait; but there was no word from Ted. Early in February, John flew to Denver on the night plane. Loren worked on correspondence until three and then retired; but she couldn't sleep. A vague uneasiness gnawed at her mind until four o'clock when the telephone rang and the uneasiness ceased to be vague.

The call was just as it had been before. No words at all—just that same gay piano serenade . . .

For the next few months, John's trips were frequent. It was the busy time of the year. On the first night of his next departure, she didn't try to sleep. At four o'clock, the telephone rang.

". . . don't sit under the apple tree with anyone else but me."

She tried having the call traced. It was useless. The caller was too clever. Clever, but purposeless. Aside from starting her nerves on a process of disintegration, the calls were inane. Ted was too practical minded to torture without a purpose. It was the kind of sadistic trick she might expect of a jealous rival.

"Celeste!"

At one minute past four, on a morning when John was planing to Omaha, Loren placed the telephone back in the cradle convinced that she'd hit upon the source of her troubles. Ted was more clever than she'd imagined. He'd gone to John Banion's ex-wife, rather than his present wife. He'd told her his story, and now Celeste was trying to break up John's marriage by torturing his wife into a breakdown. At one minute past four A.M., immediately following the fourth of the maddening calls, the scheme seemed obvious to Loren. Wear her down, weaken her, unnerve her, and then—

She wasn't quite sure what Celeste meant to do then; but there was no reason to wait and see. Two could play this game!

Loren's mind became quite clear. She began to analyze. The calls came only on the first night of John's trips. Reason: had John been at home he might have intercepted the calls. Furthermore, there was never any way of knowing how long he would be gone. The only way of avoiding him was to make the call immediately after his departure. This meant that Celeste had access to John's plans.

On the following day, Loren spoke to Katy.

"Do you remember the day the former Mrs. Banion had an interview with Mr. Banion?" she asked.

Katy considered her answer only a moment.

"Yes, I do, Mrs. Banion."

"Did she come in alone?"

This time, Katy considered a bit longer.

"I don't think I remember—yes, I do. A man came with her. He waited in the reception room."

Ted, obviously.

"Have you seen him since?"

"No, Mrs. Banion."

But there were other girls in the office—young, impressionable. Ideal bait for Ted's charms.

"Katy, I want you to do something for me. Talk to the girls, casually, of course, and try to learn if any of them has a new, dreamy boyfriend."

Katy laughed.

"According to what I pick up in the lounge, most of them have a new, dreamy boyfriend every week."

"That's not what I mean! I mean one *certain* boyfriend."

She was making a mess of it. A casual inquiry was

becoming an inquisition; but there was still one thing she must know.

"And Katy, on the day when the former Mrs. Banion had the interview with Mr. Banion, did you, by any chance, overhear anything that was said?"

"Overhear, Mrs. Banion?"

There was such a thing as being too naive, and Loren's patience had worn thin.

"Accidentally or otherwise," she snapped. "Oh, don't look so wounded. I had your job once, and I was ambitious and human. I listened; I spied. I know what goes on in an office. This is important to me, Katy. I'll make it worth your while if you can tell me anything —anything at all."

It was a foolish, weak, female thing to do, and Loren regretted her words as soon as they were spoken. Had Katy been shocked, it wouldn't have been so bad; but it was all Loren could do to suppress the desire to slap the hint of a smile she saw on Katy's face.

You're cracking up, Loren. You're losing control.

She held on tight, and Katy's smile faded.

"I'm sorry, Mrs. Banion. I didn't hear anything. But if I do hear anything, I'll let you know."

Loren went back to her office shaken at her own self-betrayal. Celeste was succeeding. Whatever her diabolical plan, she was succeeding. Never had she spoken to an employee as she had spoken to Katy. Never . . .

When John returned from Omaha, he found Loren confined to her bed.

"It's nothing," she insisted. "I think I had a touch of flu."

"You've had more than a touch of over-work," John said. "I warned you, Loren. Now I'm going to send you off on a vacation."

So Celeste can have a clear field. That's her game. It must be her game.

"No—!" Loren protested. "Not now! Not at a time like this!"

John's face became very grave. He sat down on the edge of the bed, still wearing his topcoat—his brief case and newspaper in his hand. These he placed on the bed beside her.

"You've heard, then," he said. "Loren, there's no reason to be upset. It isn't as if she meant anything to me—or had meant anything to me for years. In fact—" There were times when John's mouth hardened and became almost cruel. "—I'd be a liar if I pretended to be sorry."

The newspaper had fallen open on the bed. While she was still trying to understand John, Loren's glance dropped and was held by the photograph of a familiar face. Celeste. She drew the paper closer until she could read the story. Celeste had been in an auto accident upstate. Celeste was dead.

Celeste was dead. It was horrible to feel so happy; and impossible not to. The pressure was gone. Her diabolical scheme would never materialize. Within a few days, Loren was herself again.

Three weeks later, John flew to San Francisco. Loren worked late, as usual, retired, and slept soundly— until four o'clock in the morning when the telephone rang.

The serenade continued.

A siren was sobbing somewhere in the street below. The sound brought Loren through time back to the immediate. She snuffed out her cigarette in a now cluttered tray and her eyes found the clock again. Three forty-five. The sound of the siren faded; but now she sat upright, her heart pounding. Why was she afraid? She had been methodical and efficient and decisive. That was the important thing—decisive.

"The thing to remember about business, Miss Donell, is that an executive must learn to make decisions and stand by them. You may be right, you may be wrong —but make the decision!"

That had been John Banion instructing his new secretary—eager, ambitious, and—why not face it—already in love with her boss. It had taken six years for him to recognize that love and turn to her when he finally discovered what everyone else had known about Celeste all along; and in the meantime, Loren had learned to be decisive.

Decisive. The first four o'clock call after Celeste's death removed all doubts. It was Ted; and it was her move. But where was Ted? It would have been easy enough to trace Celeste; but Ted was another matter. She didn't want to use a private investigator and leave a trail that could be traced. The solution to her problem came from an unexpected source: Katy.

"Mrs. Banion, do you recall asking about the man who was with the former Mrs. Banion when she came to the office just before Christmas?"

It was two weeks after Celeste's death. Loren didn't look up from her desk; she mustn't betray her excitement.

"What about him?" she asked casually.

"It's a peculiar coincidence; but I had to run an errand for Mr. Banion across town yesterday, and I saw the man. He was going into a small hotel—The Lancer. I think he must live there. He had a bundle under his arm that looked like laundry."

"You're very observant," Loren said dryly.

"You did ask—"

Loren looked up, smiling.

"Ancient history," she said, "but thanks, anyway. You're a diligent girl."

Loren wasn't so casual later when she drove to the Lancer Hotel, parked across the street and watched the entrance until she saw Ted come out. It was a shabby hotel in a shabby neighborhood; Celeste hadn't, obviously, contributed much to Ted's economic security. This wasn't a condition Ted could long endure. She watched him walk from the hotel to a bowling alley at the end of the block, and then went into a drug store phone booth to verify his registration at the hotel. That done, she went to work.

The first thing to be done was to obtain a recording of a piano solo of Ted's theme. This, for a small fee, was easily accomplished. For a somewhat larger fee, she then obtained a small wire recorder of a type that could be carried in a handbag or a coat pocket. At home, she transferred the record onto the tape, adding a personal touch at the conclusion:

"We can reach an understanding if you will meet me behind the bowling alley at 2 A.M."

She destroyed the record and put the wire recorder away until John's next business trip. On the first Thursday in March, he took the night plane to Chicago. As soon as she knew he was leaving, Loren did two things: she recorded two hours of correspondence on the dictating machine in her bedroom, and reserved two tickets at a playhouse.

Katy begged off from the theatre.

"I'd love to, Mrs. Banion, but it's the wrong night. You see, I have a friend—"

"Then hang on to him," Loren said. "A good man's hard to find. I'll ask someone else."

An out of town customer had nothing to do for the

evening. Anyone was acceptable as long as she had a companion. She drove to the theatre in her own car. During the first intermission, she excused herself and went to a telephone booth in the lobby. She took the wire recorder from her bag, dialed Ted's hotel, and waited for his voice. As soon as he answered, she switched on the recorder and held it to the mouthpiece. When the recording was concluded, she hung up the telephone, replaced the recorder in her bag, and returned to her place in the theatre.

It was twelve-thirty, when Loren returned to her apartment the first time. She left her car parked in the street, as she frequently did after the garage attendant had gone off duty. It was safe. Every hour on the hour, Officer Hanlon made his rounds. She wanted the car to be seen. In the lobby, she met other theatre and party going tenants returning home, and rode up in the elevator with them. She went directly to her room and put the wire recorder away in the drawer of the work table in her bedroom, transferring the gun to her handbag in its place. Then she set up the dictating machine, opened the bedroom windows enough to make certain the words would be heard on the deck below and waited until exactly one o'clock before turning on the machine. It was time to go.

She went down in the service elevator and left the building through the alley—unseen. She didn't take the car. She walked a distance and caught a cab, took the cab to within six blocks of Ted's hotel and walked the rest of the way. At two o'clock, she was waiting in the shadows behind the bowling alley. Ted was only a few minutes late. He advanced close enough for her to see the surprised recognition in his eyes before she fired. A strike in the bowling alley covered the shots. Ted fell and didn't move again. When she was certain that he

was dead, Loren walked away—not hurriedly, but at
a normal pace. The streets were almost empty at
this hour, but within a few blocks she found a cab,
rode to within six blocks of her apartment, and
walked the rest of the way. The service entrance was
locked, but the front lobby was empty.

It was exactly ten minutes before three when Loren
returned to her apartment . . .

. . . The sound of the siren faded away, but not the
pounding of Loren's heart. It was as if she had been in
a kind of sleepwalker's trance, and now she became
horribly aware of the fact that she was a murderess. The
horror didn't lie in the fact that Ted was dead—she
cared no more for that than John had cared about
Celeste's death. It was something else. Fear—but what
could go wrong? She'd been at the theatre, with an escort, when the hotel switchboard had handled Ted's
call. She'd left her windows open so Cherry Morgan
could hear her voice. She'd left her car on the street, and
come up in the elevator with friends. She'd destroyed
the record—The wire recorder. Loren was out of bed
in an instant. She ripped open the table drawer, opened
the recorder, and pulled free the wire. She wiped it
clean on the skirts of her negligee. No evidence. There
was no way to connect her with the body the police
would find behind a bowling alley in a shabby neighborhood across town; but there must be no evidence. The wire was clean. What else? Katy had told
her where to find Ted; but she didn't even know his
name. John—? No matter what Celeste might have
told John, he would never connect her with Ted's
murder.

But the gun. She should have gotten rid of the gun.
She snatched it out of the handbag and began to look
about for a hiding place. The echo of the police siren

was still in her ears, and reason wouldn't still it. The gun was the one damning piece of evidence. She stood with it in her hands, turning about, directionlessly— and the doorbell rang.

When Loren went to the door, it was with a gun in her hands and doom in her mind. Just in time, she remembered to stuff the weapon under a cushion of the divan, and then go on to open the door. Officer Hanlon stood in the lighted hall looking all of nine feet tall.

"Mrs. Banion," he said, "I'm sure sorry to disturb you at this hour, but there was no one on duty downstairs."

She couldn't speak a word. Not one.

"I didn't know where to leave this."

He held up a set of keys, dangling them before her eyes. It was some seconds before she recognized them.

"You left them in your car, Mrs. Banion. I noticed the window was down when I went past at one o'clock, but I didn't think I could do anything about it without some way to turn on the ignition. It started to sprinkle a few minutes ago, so I stopped to see what I could do. I found these. You're getting careless, Mrs. Banion."

Loren saw her hand reach out and take the keys; it might have been detached from her body.

"Thank you," she said. "Is that all?"

"That's all, Mrs. Banion. Sorry to get you out of bed, but I didn't know what else to do."

Loren closed the door, then leaned against it—listening until she could hear Hanlon go down in the elevator. Only the keys? She wanted to laugh, and she wanted to cry. Most of all, she wanted John. She wanted to cling to him, to bury her head on his shoulder and be safe. The weeks of terror were over, and all Hanlon had wanted was to give her the keys! John was gone, but his room was next to hers. She ran to it, turned on the light, and went to the chair behind his desk. Soft, rich leather with the feel of John in it—the contour of his back, the worn places where he'd gripped the arm rests. And then Loren's eyes fell on the desk. For a moment, she was afraid John had gone off without his ticket. The airline envelope was there. She looked inside. The ticket was gone. *I'm becoming a neurotic woman who worries about everything,* she thought. And then she noticed what was written on the envelope in the time of departure line: 8:00 A.M. 1/6/.

The sixth was Friday. 8:00 A.M. *was in the morning. This morning—not Thursday night.*

It had to be a mistake. The airline office was open all night. She dialed quickly.

"John Banion? . . . What flight did you say? No, there was no John Banion on the nine o'clock flight to Chicago . . . The eight o'clock this morning? . . . Yes. We have a reservation for John Banion . . . Who is this calling? . . . Oh, Mrs. Banion. Your husband flies with us frequently. He always takes the daytime flights. Always."

Loren put the telephone back on John's desk, and stood listening to the words of a story. It had begun with John's fingers digging into her arms.

"I couldn't stand being fooled again!" he'd said.

And then, on the day Celeste had come to see him—
"Loyalty," John said. *"It's a word. Just a word."*

"Oh, no, John," Loren whispered.

"I like to fly at night," John said. *"It's smoother and I—"*

"John, no—"

But it had to be John. He'd seen her face that day in Miami when Ted played an old melody. He'd gotten some story from Celeste—enough of a story to induce him to buy her silence, and immediately afterwards the calls had begun. And where was John when he didn't take the night flights he was supposed to take? With a cold certainty, Loren knew. Men lived by patterns. He had turned to his secretary once, and now— hadn't Katy been the one who had told her where to find Ted? Katy, who couldn't go to the theatre because she was expecting a friend? Katy, that not so naive child who *did* listen at the boss' door . . .

And Ted Lockard was dead. Loren remembered that when the telephone in her bedroom started ringing. She turned and walked slowly and obediently into her room. She picked up the telephone and listened to the music with an expressionless face. It was four o'clock. It was time for John's serenade.

A TALE OF 5 G's
by C. B. Gilford

Maybe he should have known better, and in fact he was uneasy. He was a lawyer, and he should have known that in a pay-off you're taking a first step without being able to predict what the last step is going to be. If a client had asked him about the wisdom of the kind of thing he himself was doing now, he probably would have advised against it. But then it's simple to sit behind a desk and hand out sage advice when you're not directly, emotionally, involved in the problem. But it's quite different, and not nearly so simple, when the stake is personal, when you're trying to protect someone who's important to you. And especially when that someone is a woman.

"Five thousand in one hundreds, right, Mr. Hannon?" the teller asked him. The teller was a mousy girl with big, horn-rimmed glasses. Five thousand in cash, drawn from an account which didn't contain much more than that, was a respectable sum.

"That's right, fifty bills," he answered. She counted them. Then he watched her slip them into a brown envelope and hand it to him under the bars. He took the envelope, transferred it immediately, almost guiltily, to his inside pocket, and walked quickly out of the bank.

It was only two blocks from there to his destination.

Dominic's Bar was a little mahogany-paneled place, a businessmen's daytime rendezvous. His man was waiting for him, in a booth toward the rear. Hannon walked to him, put his hand into his inner pocket without sitting down. "I have the money, Trask," he said.

The other man smiled up and said, "Join me in a drink, Mr. Hannon."

"No, thanks."

The man looked offended, and his smile grew narrower. "Hannon," he said, "I'm doing you a favor. Let's be friendly about this or the deal's off."

Hannon sat down. He didn't want to call any more attention to this transaction than he had to.

"What do you drink, Mr. Hannon?" Trask questioned him.

"Bourbon."

Mel Trask conveyed the selection to a passing waiter, then turned back grinning. He was a dark-complexioned man with dog-like brown eyes, wavy hair, and gleaming white teeth that were displayed prominently when he grinned. He was middle-sized, trim and athletic, with wide shoulders and a well-muscled leanness. A ladies' man strictly. A small-time hood without great talent or brains, but just clever enough to realize that the only real talent he did have was his ability to attract women.

"Well, Mr. Hannon, you've decided you love your wife five thousand dollars' worth." His voice was as smooth and suave as his looks. "But I hope you understand one thing. This five grand guarantees only that I move out of Alix's life. It doesn't guarantee that she'll go back to you."

"Yes, I realize that."

"So you're not betting on a sure thing."

"I told you I realize that."

The waiter came and set a glass in front of Hannon. Trask lifted his own glass as if for a toast and sipped from it. "But it's not a bad gamble," he said, "even against heavy odds. Alix is quite a girl. I'd say it ought to be worth the money to you just to get the field clear so you can make another try."

"Trask, let me worry about that."

"Okay, Hannon, but there's one thing we didn't agree on. How long is this deal for?"

Hannon tensed. "What do you mean?" he asked cautiously.

"Well, with me out of the way you're going to try to get Alix back. But suppose you flub it? Suppose she doesn't take you back? Let's say I give you three months, and you're still on the outside. You've had the chance you paid for, and I ought to be able to move back in."

Hannon tried to put it carefully. "You don't get my point, Trask. I'm not buying Alix from you for five thousand. I'm paying five thousand so she can get rid of you. Like she has a toothache, and I pay a dentist to get rid of it for her."

Trask shrugged, finished his drink, then put both his hands on the table. "Give me the money, Hannon," he said softly.

The transfer of the envelope was made with quick, furtive movements. Trask put the envelope in an inner pocket too. Then he edged out of the booth and stood up. "But a toothache sometimes comes back," he said, and walked out.

Hannon was left with the bar check, his own fury, and the unpleasant feeling he'd had before—that maybe he'd have been wiser leaving things as they were, and that he didn't know what he had started, nor how it would all end.

It had been entirely his own fault, of course. He realized that bitterly again as he woke up to a new day.

It was always like this, always the worst the first thing in the morning. Perhaps it was because his subconscious stubbornly persisted in believing that he was going to wake some day and find that Alix's leaving him was nothing but a bad dream, and Alix herself was still in the room, her head on the pillow next to his.

The room—the whole apartment—was still full of her. When she had gone, he hadn't touched or changed anything. First, because he had imagined that she would reconsider and be back soon. Then finally because he wanted to punish himself with the living memory of her, and the evidences and reminders of her occupancy were that punishment. She hadn't asked him to send her the few personal effects she had overlooked in her quick departure, and he'd kept them. The odd items that lingered in drawers and stared up at him accusingly when he chanced upon them, her boudoir table with its mirrors now empty of her reflection, the bottle of perfume whose genie he let loose from its prison now and then to waft the scent of Alix through the rooms —there were a hundred things. But all her. All his wife.

He missed her. He still loved her. And he wanted her back. He must have been insane. No matter the excuses. No matter what might be called the extenuating circumstances. All right, Alix had been out of town while he and Chrys Waring had been working so hard on the McCalmon case. All right, he hadn't known that all the time Chrys had been in love with him. She'd been a wonderful secretary, and she'd really helped on the McCalmon case. Then the verdict came in and McCalmon was acquitted, and he had taken Chrys out to dinner to celebrate. Chrys was mighty attractive. They'd had a few drinks, and he'd taken her for a drive. There hadn't been much more to it than that. Not completely innocent, but not quite as bad as it looked either. But he'd been stupid to let it happen. And he'd been stupid to be in a place with Chrys Waring where he could be seen and recognized.

No, getting rid of Mel Trask couldn't change the past.

But the whole Trask business had been his fault too. Indirectly, but still his fault. If Alix hadn't been out on her own, she'd have never gotten mixed up with any other man. If she hadn't wanted deliberately to spite her husband, she'd never have consorted with such a potentially dangerous man as Mel Trask. Alix had started off on her career of independence by taking up with a bohemian crowd, a bunch of screwballs who thought that going to places where the criminal element consorted was intriguing and exciting. Alix had been just the sort to catch the attention of Mel Trask, for she was a beautiful woman, an estranged wife, and the wife of an up-and-coming criminal lawyer at that.

Yes, his fault completely. Now he was merely trying to unwind and untangle what had become so wound up and tangled.

He got up listlessly, dressed and shaved, wondering what he should do next. At the office, Nancy Dillon greeted him with her shy, careful smile. Nancy was a very plain girl who knew her place because she knew precisely why she'd been hired. She brought him the file on the Overton case and he spent the morning on that. Or at least he tried to concentrate on it. At one o'clock he went out for lunch.

That was when he saw the noon editions. They reported that Mel Trask, a local hoodlum with a police record, had been shot to death.

Hugh Hannon lived by the newspapers for the next two days. In a way, of course, he was relieved that Trask was dead. A dead man wouldn't return for a second payoff. And he didn't care who had killed Trask. The person he was concerned about was Alix.

But the papers made no mention of her. They furnished a pretty complete biography of Trask, his three arrests and one conviction for extortion, his known connections with the Rossiter gang, his friendships with nightclub performers like Gale Gray and Lisa Norman. He was sure if any reporter had discovered the deceased's relationship with Alix Hannon, the news would have been used with a vengeance. Because that would make a political story worth a headline in itself. The wife of Hugh Hannon, maybe next State's Attorney-General, definitely a young man with a future —the wife of *that* Hugh Hannon mixed up in an unpleasant way with a cheap hoodlum. So the fact they didn't print that juicy little item proved that they didn't have it.

And that meant that Trask hadn't boasted about Alix to anyone. That puzzled Hannon. Of course there were several possible answers. Maybe the best was that Trask had had faith in Hugh Hannon's political future. If Hugh Hannon ever achieved any high office, the fact of an old friendship with Mrs. Hannon might be good leverage for a favor. A friendship that was common knowledge wouldn't be worth anything, but a secret friendship could have real value. Some reasoning like that was just like Trask. He'd been a hoodlum who had operated by unconventional methods.

Where, though, was the five thousand dollars? No mention was made of that either. One of the main reasons that robbery was ascribed as the motive for the killing was the fact, duly noted by the police, that no money was found on the corpse. Maybe it was robbery, Hannon thought. But he wasn't going to volunteer the information that the missing money totaled at least five grand.

He had disturbed moments, of course. If robbery had been the motive, then he himself had by coincidence supplied the motive to Trask's killer. The net effect was the same as if he'd paid someone five thousand to murder Trask.

On the third day after the crime, the papers reported that the police had arrested a suspect. He was a small-time crook named Phil Cooley.

Later that same day, Hugh Hannon got a phone call. Phil Cooley wanted him to come down to the city jail to see him.

Hannon had never met or heard of Phil Cooley—before reading of his arrest—so when the uniformed sergeant ushered him into the cell, he was both anxious and curious to see who was being accused of murdering Mel Trask. He found a small weasel of a man, not more than five-six and a hundred and thirty pounds, with a thin, pinched face, doleful gray eyes, and lank, straight brown hair that fell over his ears and forehead. Or rather those were his normal features. Added to them at the moment were a number of bruises, a swollen lip, a discolored left eye, and a couple of bandages that must have covered cuts and lacerations.

"I'm Hugh Hannon," Hannon announced himself.

Cooley offered a limp hand. "Sure, I know who you are, Mr. Hannon," he said with a fawning tone and attitude. "I've seen your picture in the papers."

"Well, I don't know you," Hannon told him.

"I'm Phil Cooley. I shot Mel Trask."

Hannon tried not to show any particular surprise at the other's frankness. "You've been arrested as a suspect," he corrected him.

"Oh, sure. But I did shoot Trask."

"All right, if you say so."

"I need a lawyer, Mr. Hannon. You're the best there is."

"You don't need the best lawyer if you shot him and you're admitting it."

"But I want to get off. It was self-defense."

The little man smiled in a peculiar way. Not just peculiar because the cuts and bruises and the swollen lip made the smile twist diagonally across his face. But there was a quality in the smile, maybe conspiratorial, maybe just secretive and superior. Whatever it was, Hannon didn't like it.

"Do you want to tell me what happened, Mr. Cooley?" he asked.

"Are you my lawyer or not?"

"I claim the privilege of not deciding till I know what I'm up against. It has to be that way."

They sat side by side on Cooley's bunk. Cooley smoked, calmly, deliberately, but Hannon refused the offer of a cigarette.

"Let's start with me," Cooley began. He wasn't a completely uneducated man like some of his type. He probably could have made an honest living if he'd tried, but he was one of those men who have been born with warped mentalities and turn naturally to criminal occupations. "I've got a record, Mr. Hannon, only it's the kind that won't help me in a trial for murder. A little forcible entry and burglary, sometimes running errands for the big boys, making a little book, mostly on my own. That's how Mel Trask owed me two hundred."

"A gambling debt?"

"That's right. He owed me that for maybe a month. I asked him for it a couple of times, and he always said he didn't have the dough. He wasn't in any hurry with me, you see, because he knew it was my own book, so he didn't owe it to any of the big boys. Then I ran into him the other night, and he was loaded. With dough I mean. He not only said he was, but I saw him flash his wad. It was at Tomaso's and Trask was buying drinks for a couple of broads. I asked him for my two hundred, and he told me to get lost. Now I didn't mind so much when he was broke, or even when he just said he was broke. But it gets me when I see he has it and won't pay off. So I kept asking him. I stayed with Trask right up to his apartment. You see, when he passed out, I was going to peel two bills off that wad of his."

"No more than that?" Hannon asked sharply.

Cooley smiled again. In profile the smile was even more grotesque. It ran into the swollen side of his mouth, puffed it up further like an ugly, misshapen balloon. "Who knows what I would have done if I'd got the chance?" he asked. "But I didn't get the chance. Trask didn't pass out for me. He just stayed nasty. He told me to get out of his apartment. I said I wasn't getting out till I had my dough. Then he started on me."

Cooley snubbed out his cigarette and turned his face around to Hannon. The face had absorbed a real beating. There was no question about that.

"Trask was a lot bigger than me," Cooley said. "And pretty good with his fists. At first I just tried to get out of the apartment but Trask wouldn't let me go. He dragged me back a couple of times. I looked around for something I could grab and hit him back with, but he was always too fast for me. Then I saw he had a gun inside his coat. I got hold of it. I was going to just back him away with it. I didn't want to shoot him. But as I was pulling the gun out, he grabbed for it too. Since it was pointing toward him when it went off, he got the slug instead of me, and that finished Trask."

Hannon glanced away from the damaged face and considered what he'd heard for a moment. Cooley's story matched up pretty well with the newspaper accounts. Trask's apartment had shown ample evidence of a struggle. And ballistics had proved that Trask had been shot with his own gun, which had been found on the rug beside the corpse.

"How did they track you down, Cooley?" he wanted to know.

"My prints were on the gun. I was too mixed up and scared to think about wiping them off. They checked prints in their files and found mine."

"You didn't try to get out of town."

"No, I just hid out. But they found me."

"Did you tell them about the fight with Trask?"

"I told 'em nothing. They'd have hauled me in whatever I told 'em."

"All right, but you've got the injuries to prove the fight."

"This face ought to prove something." Cooley grinned.

"It shouldn't be too hard then to make a self-defense plea stick."

"Except for one thing, Mr. Hannon." Cooley lit a second cigarette slowly.

"What's that?"

"The money."

"What money? Your two hundred?"

"No, the five thousand."

Hannon got a sick feeling then. He'd forgotten for the moment about the five thousand. But did it make a difference to the cause of justice *where* Trask had got hold of that five grand? Did the world have to know Hugh Hannon had paid it to him to stay away from his wife?

"You mean Trask's five thousand?" Hannon asked too quickly.

"Why do you say Trask's five thousand?"

"You said Trask had a big wad."

"But I didn't say how much."

"All right, you didn't say."

"I don't know how much Trask had on him."

"All right, so you don't know."

"I mean my five thousand, Mr. Hannon. That was just about how much I had when the cops picked me up."

"Where did you get hold of five grand? You said you were arguing with Trask over a mere two hundred."

"That's right. But I'd been doing pretty good for myself. That's where I got the five grand. Not all at once. Been saving it up. Is it any crime to have five grand?"

"Not in itself, no."

"But it's the kind of thing to make the cops suspicious, you know."

"What about all the money Trask had?"

"I didn't touch it, Mr. Hannon."

"The papers have never said anything about any money being found on the corpse. So I'm presuming there wasn't any. Yet you say he was flashing a wad. Now what happened to it?"

"How should I know? Look, Mr. Hannon, I left a corpse behind me in that apartment in the middle of the night, maybe two or three o'clock. They found the body about eight o'clock in the morning. Five or six hours in between. Anybody could have grabbed Trask's dough. Lots of people saw him flashing it. Then there was the maid who found him. Or some of the cops even."

Hannon didn't like the sound of it but he couldn't prove it wasn't so. "We'll pass that by for the moment," he said. "Is there anything else you want to tell me?"

Cooley screwed up his ugly little face into a thoughtful expression. "Like what, Mr. Hannon?"

Hannon tried to make his next question sound objective, impersonal. "Did Trask tell you where he got his money in the first place?"

The sly smile flitted back onto Cooley's face. "Well, sort of. When we first got up to his apartment, you see, he didn't start hitting me right away. He was kind of drunk like I said, and started bragging. Said he had a new little racket. He said it wasn't the racket for a poor, ugly dope like me. He said a guy had to have looks and brains to work his racket."

"And what was his racket?"

"Women. Married women. Said he had several married women on the string, and one of the husbands had just paid off. Paid Trask to stay away from his wife, that is."

Hannon took a deep, slow breath folded his arms across his chest to hide his hands, so Cooley wouldn't see that they were trembling. "Did he give you the name of this particular husband?"

Cooley didn't answer for a moment. The two men faced each other. Hannon tried to read the other's pale eyes. He didn't like what he thought he read in them.

"No, he didn't tell me the name," Cooley finally said.

"Then what he did tell you isn't much help," Hannon commented. "But the money angle is a problem. Trask's disappearing wad and your five thousand."

Cooley grinned. "I know," he said. "If it was going to be easy, I wouldn't have called for you, Mr. Hannon. But look I said I've got five grand. It's yours if you take the case. Every cent I've got."

Hannon felt that prickly sensation again. He'd paid Trask five thousand and he'd had misgivings. Now Cooley, who'd admittedly killed Trask, was offering him five thousand. And it could be the same money.

Hannon left Cooley without giving him a definite yes or no. He had to think it over, he told the little man truthfully.

Hannon had plenty to think over. First, to decide how much of the truth Cooley had told him. Had Cooley actually killed Trask in self-defense? Cooley had been beat up all right, and unless somebody else could prove the contrary, the beating had been administered by Trask. Mel Trask had been a nasty customer, capable of almost anything. So when Cooley said that Trask would have killed him, Hannon could believe it.

But the real problem was whether to defend Cooley at all. Ethically, maybe he could. There was every reason to believe Cooley was telling the truth, concerning the circumstances of the shooting at least. It didn't seem very likely that Cooley had shot Trask, deliberately in cold blood, with premeditation. Therefore, Cooley would be technically innocent of a charge of murder —if that was going to be the charge.

And the police hadn't seemed to have uncovered Trask's relationship with Alix. What would happen to her if they did? Purely aside from considerations of Hugh's career, that is. She'd undoubtedly be called as a witness in the trial. Hannon had enemies in the prosecutor's office. They'd find some excuse for putting Alix on the stand. Hannon shuddered at the thought of the questions they'd ask her, and the answers she'd have to give.

And then, finally, it occurred to him that the decision which now confronted him was the best excuse he'd had for a long time to try to see her. So he grabbed the phone quickly, before he lost his courage.

She'd moved to an apartment of her own in the Shelley Plaza. Her telephone number wasn't in the directory yet, but he knew it anyway, had memorized it from the countless times he'd wanted to call her, and hadn't dared to. He dialed the number now, listened to three rings. Then her voice came. "Hello."

"This is Hugh," he said quickly. "I've got to talk to you right away. It's very important. About Mel Trask."

She was silent for a few seconds. And for the first time it occurred to him to wonder how Trask's death had affected her. She might have actually liked Trask, and be mourning for him!

"What about Mel?" Her voice was beautiful music to his ears, but her choice of words was like a knife thrust into him. Not "Trask" or "Mel Trask," but "Mel."

"I can't talk about it over the phone," he said. "But it's important to you, Alix, so for Pete's sake, don't be difficult."

She was silent again, reluctant. He knew her dilemma. "All right," she said finally.

"I'm coming right over," he told her.

He hung up, without giving her a chance to object, rushed downstairs and hailed a cab. It was ten minutes to the Shelley Plaza. On the way he tried to rehearse what he was going to say to her. But then he gave up the attempt as being of no use. He knew he'd forget whatever he'd planned when he saw her.

Her apartment was on the third floor. He didn't wait for the elevator, but raced up the stairs, then had to stand around in front of her door for a couple of minutes so he wouldn't seem too breathless and overawed at the sight of her. But then he rang and she opened the door almost immediately, and he was breathless and overawed anyway.

He hadn't forgotten what his wife looked like, but yet this was like seeing her for the first time. The cameo skin, the misty green-blue eyes, the coppery hair like a desert sunset were all new and wonderful to him.

"Come in, Hugh," she said. Her voice was low, tight, not like her voice had once been.

He went into the little living room but he didn't sit. Alix closed the door and faced him, letting a distance of ten feet separate them.

"What is it you have to tell me?" she asked. There was to be no exchange of civilities, just business. But looking at her, he wondered. He'd been her husband. Didn't seeing him again do anything to her? She was being so careful, so controlled. Was she afraid of her own weakness?

"You knew," he began, trying to match her coolness, "that I knew about you and Trask."

"Yes, Mel told me he had talked to you. He said you'd located where I lived and you had seen him bring me home one night."

"I guess you were pretty fond of Trask," he said.

She glanced at him defiantly. "Mel was a friend," she said. "Let's let it go at that. Now what did you come here to tell me?"

"You must have read that a man named Phil Cooley was arrested for Trask's murder. Cooley has asked me to defend him."

"And you want my permission, or just what?"

"No, I just want some information from you. There have been names in the papers, names of people who were connected with Trask. But not your name. Was your friendship with Trask a secret?"

She answered reluctantly. "Yes, it was a secret. Mel wanted it that way. He said there was another woman chasing him. He didn't give me the details. So we didn't see each other too often." She acted almost as if she hated to admit this to him, and he didn't know why she did admit it. Had he exaggerated the relationship between Alix and Mel Trask? Maybe it hadn't been anything serious after all. Maybe Trask's insinuations and his own imagination had manufactured the whole thing. A dozen new explanations as to why Alix took up with Trask occurred to him now. Because Trask was different . . . and she was bored . . . she wanted to spite her husband . . . she had wanted to play with fire, but had had no real intention of plunging in . . . who could say what motivates a woman when she reacts to a big emotional blow? There might still be hope. . . .

"Look," he blurted out, "if I defend Cooley at all, my main reason will be to keep your name from being associated with Trask."

She laughed suddenly. Her laughter startled him. That she should laugh at all . . . and laughter with that quality, mocking, derisive . . .

"Darling," she said, "you can't fool me for one moment. You're worried about my name because for a little while yet it's still your name. So you're worried that you'll never get to the state capitol if the sacred name of Hannon is mentioned in the wrong connection."

He was stung by her accusation. "You won't give me

credit for anything, will you?" he said. "And you refuse to believe that I still love you."

Her eyes flashed. "Don't talk about love," she flung at him. "You're getting ready to defend the man who killed someone who loved me."

That was too much somehow. "Do you know something?" he said. "The day Mel Trask was killed he accepted five thousand dollars from me to stay away from you."

He hadn't meant to tell her that. It had slipped out because he was angry, because he was hurt, and—yes—because he loved her. But now he regretted having said it. He saw the genuine surprise on her face. She had really believed that Mel Trask had been fond of her. It's easy enough for a beautiful woman to believe that any man is fond of her. And now she had been betrayed. Maybe she had loved Trask . . .

"Five thousand," she echoed softly, numbly. "You tried to buy me for five thousand?"

"No," he said. But how could he explain? "It's a fact I paid Trask five thousand dollars. But I didn't mean to tell you about it. And I'm sorry. All we seem to be able to do is hurt each other. Good-bye, Alix. I won't try to see you any more."

And he wondered, as he walked back down to the street, if her pride had been injured simply because the price agreed upon between him and Trask had been so small, a mere five thousand.

"Five thousand isn't exactly chicken-feed, Mr. Hannon," Cooley said, puffing on a cigarette. He was leaning back on one elbow, his eyes narrowed. He almost seemed bored. And his manner was definitely an indication of his confidence.

"I've collected bigger fees," Hannon answered.

"That's funny, Mr. Hannon. I thought five thousand was a sum that would interest you."

There was a hint of a threat, ever so subtle, in Cooley's voice. How much *did* he know? He'd be too smart to try frank and open blackmail, because if he was familiar with the profession of law, he'd realize Hannon couldn't ethically accept the case under threat of blackmail. So Cooley would know he'd have to hint, to suggest, to communicate his threat without having to state it in so many words.

But was it blackmail anyway? How could he be sure? Hannon wrestled with his problem while Cooley watched him with that narrowed gaze. Maybe it was better to accept before it came to an open threat of blackmail. He was taking the case to keep Alix out of the spotlight anyway, wasn't he?

"All right," he said finally. "I'll defend you, Cooley, and the fee will be five thousand."

The area of conflict in the trial was quickly drawn. Vince Barrioz, the chief prosecutor who directed the state's case himself, did not dispute the proof that the defendant had been viciously beaten by the deceased. Although the passage of several months had healed Phil Cooley's injuries, photographs and the testimony of two physicians established the basic fact of such injuries. Also the companion fact that, aside from the fatal bullet wound, the corpse had sustained no such damage.

"The state concedes," Barrioz told the court, "that the deceased, Mel Trask, did on the night of April fourteenth, inflict these injuries on the defendant, Philip Cooley."

Also quickly established were such matters as the ballistics proof that Trask was killed by a bullet fired from his own gun, and the fact that Philip Cooley's fingerprints had been found on said gun. The whole contest, recognized by counsel on both sides, was over the money.

It was on the second day of the trial, that Hugh Hannon discovered the presence of his wife—legally his former wife now—as a spectator in the courtroom. He hadn't seen her since that nightmarish day when a judge had decreed her divorce. But as though drawn by a magnet—or maybe he half expected to see her there—his eyes swept the courtroom and fastened upon that sun-burst of her hair. For a few minutes, he didn't even hear what Barrioz and the witness were saying.

There was a long trail of witnesses that day. Barrioz staged them in tiresome succession, bartenders, drunks, hoodlums—but all of them with one story— Mel Trask had been toting a wad of money the night he was killed. Hugh Hannon didn't cross-examine any of them. Neither did he dispute the word of the detective who testified that there was no money on the corpse when the police found it, and searched it.

Hannon had his own parade of witnesses, whom he led before the poor jury the next day. Alix was in attendance that third day too. He went doggedly about making his point. His witnesses were the same kind of people as Barrioz's characters of the previous day, and they testified variously that Philip Cooley had certain sources of income, that they'd paid him this or that amount on this or that day, or had seen him with a certain amount of money on a certain day. Thus Hugh Hannon tried to make his point: it was possible to assume that Philip Cooley could have possessed five thousand dollars without having taken it from the deceased.

On the fourth day Alix was present again. Hannon wasn't at his best that day either. He had Cooley on the stand, relating the same story he'd originally told, making the plea of self-defense. When Barrioz cross-examined, he couldn't shake Cooley's version of the death struggle, but did better when Cooley contended that no part of his five thousand had been Trask's money. By the time Barrioz was finished, making Cooley account for his possession of the money, he had established Cooley as an individual operating outside or on the outskirts of the law and therefore not a very reliable witness. There were times when Hannon objected to Barrioz's line of questioning, but he didn't always choose the most strategic times. He felt that he wasn't doing his best job. And the fault was Alix's.

When he left the courtroom that day, he was confused and dejected. He sensed disaster somehow though he didn't know from what direction it would come or what form it would take. Then when he saw Alix in the corridor waiting for him, he thought he knew what she was going to tell him.

"Hugh, I want to talk to you," she said. He had stopped a few paces away from her, and she had walked up close to him. She was beautiful in a pale green suit.

"All right," he said. "Where do you want to talk, here or somewhere else?" This was her party. He wasn't going to suggest anything.

"I suppose some bar. If you don't mind."

"I don't mind. I could do with a drink."

He walked with her the four blocks it took to find a suitable place. They sat down opposite each other in a quiet booth.

"Hugh," she said, "the way things are going, Barrioz will get a conviction."

"That should please you," he said.

"Well, it doesn't," she told him.

He was too surprised to think clearly. He kept trying to read her face, and she kept trying to keep her thoughts from him. "Why not?" he asked, staring across at her.

"You can say 'I told you so' if you want to, but this trial has opened my eyes—about Mel Trask."

He should have felt happy, hearing her admit that. But she wasn't his wife any longer, and disillusionment wasn't going to make her return to him. "No, Trask wasn't any good," he agreed.

"And I can appreciate a little more now why you paid him off. It's really my fault Trask is dead. It's my fault Cooley is being tried for murder. It's my fault you have to defend him."

He wanted to reach across the table and take her hand, comfort her, but he didn't. "If you insist on going backwards and tracing the maneuvers of fate," he said, "none of these things would have happened if I hadn't been such a fool with Chrys Waring."

She looked down at her glass, hiding her eyes from him. "I really didn't come here to discuss the past," she said.

He waited. She'd already said more, admitted more, than he'd ever hoped for. He wasn't going to press her.

"I'm afraid of that man Cooley," she said finally.

He was surprised again. "Why?" he asked her.

"He's a smart little man, Hugh." She looked up now, her face very earnest. "Does he know where Trask got the money? Does he know that you paid it to Trask?"

"He tells me he doesn't."

"But you're not sure. That's why you took the case, isn't it? Because you were afraid Cooley knew and you didn't want him to tell. Maybe you're not admitting it to yourself, but Cooley has blackmailed you into defending him. What's he going to do if he sees the case is going against him? Or what's he going to do if the jury finds him guilty? He's going to talk. I know he is. Hugh, I don't want to see your career suffer."

"Because that's all I have left?"

"Please—please stick to the subject."

"I'd rather talk about us than Cooley."

"Cooley is the problem right now. And he's the one I want to talk about."

He tried to pretend that she wasn't beautiful, that she hadn't been his wife, that he didn't love her. He tried to pretend that she was a colleague, someone with whom one discusses a technical matter, rationally, logically.

"All right," he said, "what do we do about Cooley?"

"You get him acquitted. He's an unsavory character, but he killed Trask in self-defense. And if you get him acquitted, he won't talk."

"But I've been trying to get him acquitted."

"You haven't been doing too well."

"What am I doing wrong? I'd like to have your honest opinion."

"I was a lawyer's wife for too long not to have picked up a few things. And I think you're violating a cardinal rule."

"What's that?"

"A man is presumed innocent till proven guilty. Let Barrioz prove that. Make it clear to the jury that he isn't proving Cooley's guilt. The circumstantial evidence is in your favor. And another thing, Cooley is being tried for second-degree murder, not for robbery."

"What do you mean?"

"I mean that even if Barrioz could prove—which he can't—that Cooley did take the money from Trask after he was dead, that doesn't prove Cooley killed Trask to get the money. Maybe he's a scavenger, a jackal, but that doesn't make him a murderer. Phil Cooley would never tackle a Mel Trask to rob him, but a Phil Cooley would ransack a corpse any old time."

He stared at her, admiringly. "I could kiss you," he said.

She looked away from him again. But she didn't say that she didn't want him to kiss her.

The jury, after an overnight deliberation brought in its verdict at ten in the morning. And that afternoon Philip Cooley, a free man, came to Hugh Hannon's office. Hugh was trying to get Alix on the phone, to tell her the news and wasn't succeeding. He put down the phone in discouragement, just as Nancy Dillon peeked her head through the door and announced Cooley.

Cooley walked in with a broad smile, carefully closed the door behind him. Then he dug into a pocket, came up with a brown-paper envelope and threw the envelope on the desk. "The cops gave me back my five thousand," he said.

Hannon was not overwhelmingly interested in either Cooley or the money at the moment. But he tried to appear business-like. "You can give it to my secretary," he said. "She'll count it and take care of it."

"Don't call her in yet," Cooley said.

Hannon's finger stopped short of the buzzer. Cooley's sharp tone alerted him. He settled back into his swivel chair, waited.

"Before you start spending that money, Mr. Hannon," Cooley went on, "I got a few things to tell you." He sat down uninvited in one of the leather chairs. His fingers ran along the chair arms, as if testing and admiring their quality. Then he glanced briefly around at the other furnishings. "Nice place you got here," he commented.

"All right," Hannon said, "you've shown how polite you can be. What are the things you have to tell me?"

"You want to get right down to business, huh?"

"That's right. I have a few other clients."

"Okay, Mr. Hannon. I won't take up any more of your valuable time than necessary. So I'll tell it to you quick. When I killed Mel Trask, it wasn't in self-defense."

Hannon's mind snapped to attention. This was it. Actually, he'd been waiting for this ever since he'd first seen Phil Cooley. He'd pretended to himself it wasn't there, but his subconscious mind had known all along that it was there. Now he was going to know. And he wanted to know. The worst.

"Why wasn't it self-defense, Cooley?" He asked the question with calm curiosity. He had to be calm.

But his listener's unperturbed manner didn't disconcert Cooley. "Can I start way back?" he asked.

"Wherever you like."

"All right. Remember I said I followed Trask to his apartment, trying to collect the money he owed me, and he beat me up? Well, that much is still the truth. But it was different from there on."

"How was it different?"

"Like this. I didn't do a thing while he was beating me up. I tried to tell him, okay, he could keep my two hundred. But he didn't even hear me. He kept on hitting me till he got tired. Do you hear that, Mr. Hannon? Till he got tired. Then he sat himself down and had another drink. He'd brought home a bottle from the last bar. I was on the floor, trying to catch my breath so

I could try to get up and walk out. I was on the floor there maybe fifteen or twenty minutes. That was while Trask was having three or four more drinks. Getting drunker and drunker. And finally he just sort of went to sleep in the chair. Then I got up and walked around a little. I wasn't in such bad shape that I couldn't walk around. And Trask was there in the chair, asleep, snoring with his mouth wide open."

"So you took all the money he had on him," Hannon suggested.

"That's right," Cooley grinned. "Like I said before, just anybody could have come along and robbed a dead man. I thought I deserved the money more than anybody else, for the beating Trask gave me."

"Maybe you deserved it," Hannon said cautiously. "So you robbed him when he was drunk. Then he woke up and . . ."

Cooley laughed aloud, a malicious cackle. "You're a real defense lawyer, Mr. Hannon," he said. "Always trying to make things look better for the client than they really are. But you're wrong. When I was going through Trask's pockets for the money, I found out he had a gun on him. So I shot him."

Neither of them spoke then for a long moment. Cooley kept on grinning, enjoying his joke. Hannon was thinking hard trying to sort things out in his mind. He had half suspected that Cooley had robbed the corpse, but had never imagined, even subconsciously, that the shooting had occurred in any manner other than as part of a struggle.

"You shot him in cold blood?"

"That's right, Mr. Hannon. Not even second-degree murder, as you might say. But first-degree murder."

"But why? Why? Did you hate Trask that much for beating you up?"

"Always giving me the benefit of the doubt, ain't you, Mr. Hannon? Sure I hated Trask. But not that much. No, I killed him because it was part of a little plan I'd worked out."

Hannon didn't dare to ask what the plan was. He waited, expecting the worst now.

"You see," Cooley went on, "Trask told me about that little racket of his with married women. But he said I was too stupid and ugly to play that racket. And he was right. I was ugly, but I couldn't help that. But I didn't have to be stupid. There I was, trying all kinds of stupid little rackets, and none of 'em paid off too much. I needed a better racket. So I remembered what Trask told me about you . . ."

"About me?" Hannon blurted out.

"Yeah. Did I forget to tell you that Trask told me you were the one who paid him that five grand?"

Hannon didn't flinch. This part of it was the part he'd subconsciously suspected all along.

"So this is the way I figured, Mr. Hannon. I could kill Trask, then blackmail you. Now wait a minute, and I'll explain. Trask had told me you had drawn five grand from your bank account and paid the cash to him to stay away from your wife. And I knew who you were. You were a young man going places, and I was a guy who knew something you didn't want everybody to know. Only that something wasn't real bad. If I'd come to you and told you I knew you'd paid off Trask, you'd have kicked me out of this office. And anybody else I'd try to tell it to probably wouldn't believe me. So I had to get a better hold on you, Mr. Hannon. I had the five grand. Supposing you had given me that dough to kill Trask for you? Now that would really be something. And that's what I can tell people right now, Mr. Hannon. That you paid me five grand to kill Trask on account of he was bothering your wife, and you also promised to defend me if I was caught. Which I was."

Hannon came halfway out of his chair. "And I can tell the police that you confessed to a murder," he said.

Cooley slumped deeper into his chair, his grin getting wider. "Sure you can tell the cops," he said. "But they can't try me again for killing Trask. You know all about double jeopardy, don't you?"

Hannon's mind, like a boxer, feinted in all directions, searching for an opening, a way out. "Go ahead and spread that story, Cooley," he almost shouted. "Do you think they're going to believe you? Do you think for one minute they'd try me for hiring you to commit a murder?"

Cooley pursed his lips. "Oh, maybe it wouldn't come to a trial. Your word against mine. But it would look mighty funny, wouldn't it, you defending the man who killed a guy who was messing around with your wife? I don't know whether there'd be a trial, or if there was a trial, what would happen to you. But I do know this much. You'd be a dead duck when it came to your business or politics. You'd have to find another racket for yourself."

Cooley eased his small frame lazily out of the chair. "That's the little plan I had made up when I shot Trask. I took a little risk all right. But I knew if I could get you as my lawyer, I was pretty safe. You've got a terrific reputation."

Hannon rose to meet his enemy, but he had no weapons. "Just for the record, Cooley," he asked, "what's your price?"

The little man lifted the brown envelope from the desk top and returned it to his inside pocket. "Five thousand as a down payment," he answered. "Then a little bit more every so often. Like an installment plan.

You got talent. I think you can make enough to support both of us."

Cooley walked out of the office then, and Hugh Hannon couldn't stop him.

Hannon took the news to Alix. He waited at the door of her apartment till she came home. Then he went inside with her and told her everything.

"I knew I was doing the wrong thing," he finished, "when I gave that money to Trask. And I knew I was doing the wrong thing when I took Cooley as a client. Both were wrong things, because they were stupid and because they were immoral. And now I'm getting what I deserved. I'm trapped, caught. And you're caught with me."

"I deserve it too."

She sat on the sofa and cried. She put her face in her hands, and her shoulders trembled with sobs. He wanted to comfort her, but he had no comfort to offer her.

"I was going to come back to you," he said bitterly, "and I was going to ask your forgiveness for Chrys Waring all over again, and then I was going to propose to you again. But what can I ask you to share now? The life of a man being blackmailed? A man who never knows from one day to the next whether he's going to be able to satisfy the blackmailer's demands? That would be a great life, wouldn't it? Always under a threat . . ."

She glanced up at him suddenly. Her face was tear-stained, but there was a fierce glow in her eyes. "You've got to put a stop to it right now, Hugh," she said.

"How . . . ?"

"You paid off Trask. Now you've paid off Cooley. It can't go on forever. You might as well put a stop to it now as tomorrow, or next month, or next year."

"But what can I do? Tell the police what Cooley told me? Cooley was right. He can't be tried twice for the same crime. I can't send him to jail."

"But you don't have to pay him either. Don't pay him, Hugh. Tell him you're not going to pay him. Call his bluff."

"Alix, that man committed murder to set himself up in this little deal. He's not bluffing."

"All right, then. He'll tell his story. They won't put you on trial, but it will be the end of your career. We'll have to start all over again. But it would be better to start again now than much later."

She had said "we." Maybe it had just slipped out, but looking at her he knew she had meant it. They were in this thing together. Nothing else mattered now. Everything in between was a bad dream, Trask and Cooley and all of it. They had both made mistakes, and they would pay. But he was ready and willing to pay now.

He was anxious to know the price, and to make the payment. So he had to find Cooley. He couldn't wait for Cooley to come looking for him again.

He began his hunt before the dinner hour, and when it got close to midnight he was still searching. He was hampered by the fact that his quest took him through unfamiliar territory. But he didn't relent. Cooley was somewhere. Cooley could be found.

He didn't know the name of that last bar. He'd already been to too many of them to pay attention to names. Maybe he had gone around in circles, visiting some of the places twice. All of them looked alike, inside and out. The same dim lighting, the same haze of smoke, the same muted conversation, the same music whether it came from a live instrument or some bright-colored box. Only this last bar was different. Cooley was there.

He was sitting with two good-looking girls at a small table. One of them was a brunette, the other a dyed redhead. The coincidence struck Hugh Hannon. Cooley had found Mel Trask with two girls on the night he'd killed Trask. Only Trask had always had plenty of girls. But here was Cooley, whom Trask had called "stupid and ugly." Trask was dead, and Cooley had the girls now. And he'd always have the girls now, with that five thousand in his pocket that was only "a down payment," and with the other installments he hoped to get, next week, next month, next year . . . forever. Yes, Cooley had played a smart, tough, dangerous little game and right now he was thinking he had won.

Hannon walked over to the table. He didn't sit down. What he had to say was brief and definite. There would be no argument this time. Cooley didn't see him till he got there. Then he just stared up at him and licked his lips.

"Cooley," Hannon said, "the deal's off."

For a moment Cooley was only startled. Then a look of hatred, desperate and deadly, darkened his pale eyes. "I'll go to the D.A.," he muttered thickly.

"Go ahead," Hannon said. He was trembling, not with fear, but with a kind of sublime feeling, the certainty that at long last he was doing the right thing. His voice was unnaturally loud.

"I will. I swear it, I will."

Hannon stared at his nemesis, then turned away. He hadn't taken three steps when Cooley yelled, "Hey, come back here!"

Hannon stopped and twisted around, but he didn't obey the order. He saw Cooley standing up now, glaring at him savagely. A corner of the brown envelope peered out from the inside pocket of his jacket.

"You can keep that five thousand," he said. "I don't want to see it again. It's bad luck money, Cooley."

Hastily, guiltily, the little man grabbed at the envelope, shoved it out of sight again. He seemed to forget Hannon. He glanced fearfully around the dim room. His right hand, inside his jacket, clutched the envelope.

Hannon left him standing there, and went out.

The newspaper lay spread on the coffee table, mocking him. Like the eyes in a picture which can seem to follow one everywhere in a room, the headline pursued him relentlessly as he paced back and forth. Alix sat very still and stiff on the sofa, sometimes watching him, sometimes glancing back at the newspaper as if it were a live, malevolent thing.

"There's no use arguing with the facts," he said finally. "I've argued and compromised too long. I killed him. Because I went in there and I told everybody Cooley had five thousand dollars in his pocket. Oh sure, he helped. He made that guilty gesture that gave him away. But it was my fault. Someone followed him out of that place and cornered him in that alley. I know that's what happened. A little defenseless guy like Cooley had an envelope full of money in his pocket in a dive like that. There were probably people in there who would have committed murder for a lot less. Lord, it was a perfect setup. If I'd been trying to arrange to get rid of him, I couldn't have picked a better way. Talk about poetic justice doesn't alter facts. I killed him."

Alix nodded. "I suppose so," she said. "We both had a hand in it. Don't blame it all on yourself. What are we going to do now?"

"You know what I want to do."

"I think so."

"I've got to tell the police everything I know. Maybe I could identify those two girls he was with. They might know something. But I've got to give the police my full cooperation. In fact, I think I'd better tell them everything, right from the beginning."

He watched her, looking for a sign. "It would involve you too," he went on. "The thing would happen that I've been trying to prevent happening all this time. Your good name . . ."

She stood up, interrupting him. She walked around the coffee table where the newspaper lay. She approached him shyly, then suddenly she was in his arms, crying, and kissing him, and whispering into his ear.

"I have only one name, good or bad . . . Mrs. Hugh Hannon . . . and I want to go with you when you tell them . . ."

BLOOD WILL TELL

by Arthur Porges

"Breathes there a cop with hide so tough, he thinks
four amendments aren't enough!"

Ulysses Price Middlebie, Professor Emeritus of the
History and Philosophy of Science, and sometime consultant in criminology, smiled tightly at Sergeant Black's
doggerel. "The Fifth Amendment," he said solemnly,
"is a splendid conception, designed to prevent the taking of evidence under torture. It is no more to be
blamed for being misused than the morphine which,
instead of helping a cancer victim, gives some young
fool a thrill."

"I know," Black said. "I was just letting off steam.
It's damned frustrating to see a murderer get off scot-
free, no matter how noble the Fifth Amendment itself
might be. Besides, it isn't always clear to us cops just
how the lawyers spread that one rule so ludicrously
thin."

Middlebie sank deeper into his old leather armchair,
and fixed luminous gray eyes on the young detective.

"I'm not a lawyer," he said, "so it's not at all plain
to me what you expect here. In the purely scientific
matters of crime detection, I've been able to help you
out on several occasions. But if you're looking for
loopholes in the Fifth Amendment, I must plead a
total incapacity to offer advice."

"You have a point," Black admitted. "It's just that you are a problem-solver, and even though a legal aspect is involved, there may be some other approach I can't visualize. You might be able to succeed, judging from past performance. In any case, I'd like to discuss the situation with you—okay?"

"By all means. Your cases are usually quite interesting. Or possibly you don't bring me the other kind."

"That's right, I don't. I come to you only when I'm in a bind. I'm a pretty good detective," he added, without false modesty, "but you've made a specialty of logical deduction, and have fifty years of experience in practicing what you preach. I know it wasn't crime consultations, but more of a PhD Doctor—a man who could help almost any young research student over a bad block in his project. There isn't such a difference. Your work on past cases proves that."

"Thanks," Middlebie said drily. "But any more butter, and I'll need a serum cholesterol test!" Then he smiled in a way that removed any sting from the reproach. "I know you meant that as a sincere compliment, but it's difficult for an old curmudgeon like me to accept praise gracefully. Now, about the case—or rather," he punned outrageously, "the fifth!"

"Well, it's basically a simple matter. There's a skunk by the name of Carleton Chambers Dell—at least, that's his current one—who has almost certainly disposed of three wives for their insurance and possessions. They were murdered in other states, by the way. Now he's killed a fourth one here, and luckily for us, got a little careless. It seems that wife number four got in a good swing at his nose, which is hard to miss, and he spilled several ounces of blood at the scene of the crime. It was meant to look like an accident, but he goofed, and the death was called murder."

He paused, and Middlebie asked: "Where does the Fifth Amendment come in? It would seem to be a clear case of First Degree Homicide."

"Ordinarily, yes, but Dell has the luck of the Devil. There are several possible suspects he didn't know existed, but we turned them up—not with any intention of helping him, you can bet! Just part of the routine investigation before we even knew about Dell's past record. In other words, we don't have a sure case against him—one that will really stand up in court, and against his lawyer, who's about the best around. As to the Fifth Amendment, did you know that it applies in this state to a blood test? That is, we can't force Dell to give us a sample of his blood. That pool near the victim undoubtedly came from his nose, which was known to be red and bruised the morning after the murder. It's the rarest type, the police lab says, and if we could state in court that Dell's blood is a match, I think we'd have him, because the other suspects are all different."

"I should think the elimination ought to be enough," Middlebie said.

"Not with Parks, his lawyer. He'll bring in another unknown killer and confuse the issue. Mrs. Dell was a weird one, and had a lot of off-beat friends. One of them *might* have done it."

"Are you sure it didn't happen that way?"

"Morally, yes, because of his past record. But we can't use that during the trial; that's never permitted. Plus the fact that he's obviously scared to death about giving any blood. He's claimed everything from religious objections—and he has about as much religion as the late Stalin—down to the Fifth Amendment. That did it. The court has warned us not to touch his sacred veins, or else."

"I suppose," Middlebie said, a wicked glint in his eyes, "you couldn't manage to have somebody, quite casually, punch his nose in public?"

"I thought of that," Black admitted ruefully. "But we'd be crucified in court. They'd make a martyr out of Dell. Too many complaints about abuse of police power these days. Some of it is justified," he added hastily, "but cops are human, and they like shortcuts as well as the next guy. When you see some punk sneering at the law, and practically daring you to make something stick, it's hard to remember civil liberties. That's not an excuse; just an explanation."

"We should all be careful about criticizing anybody until we've worn his shoes a few days," Middlebie said. "But surely Dell must have an army record, complete with blood type."

"Not that we can find. My guess is he ducked that one just as easily as he's ducked the law. Hid out in Mexico, faked a disease, or got an 'essential' job through bribery or pull—who knows?"

"What about hospitalization?"

"Nothing. Either he's in perfect health, or, more likely, used a phony name. So you see what I'm up against. No blood, no solid case. Either I let him go without bringing a murder charge, or pull him in, and risk losing in court because there's no proof that blood came from his big, bunged-up nose."

Middlebie was silent for a moment, his eyes blank. After a few moments he said: "Then I take it that if— and mind you I only say 'if'; I don't know how it could be done—but if you could get some of his blood without violence, even through fraud, you'd have your case."

"Provided we could prove in court our sample really came from Dell. Which means good, dependable med-

ical evidence in the form of some reputable doctor."
Black's face was grim. "It's a hopeless problem. Blood
without violence. He's so cautious now that if Albert
Schweitzer wanted to nick him for any reason, Dell
would refuse automatically. Nobody's going to get any
of his blood voluntarily, that's certain. And we can't
take it by force. So I guess I've bent your ear for nothing. The problem can't have a solution."

"At the moment, I'd have to agree," the professor
said. "But let me sleep on it. Occasionally an impossible
problem has an obvious answer."

Black looked at him in wonder.

"You mean there might be a chance?" He shook his
head several times. "You never say 'die,' do you? Well,
I know better than to bet against you, but I can't see a
way out of this mess." He paused at the door. "Here's
hoping I hear from you tomorrow."

"Wonderful stuff, blood," Middlebie said absently.
"No wonder so many people hate the idea of losing any.
I don't mean criminals, like Dell," he added. Then, with
more resolution in his voice, "We can't let this wife-
killer get away with only a punch in the nose!"

"He will, if you don't stop him," Black retorted, and
left.

When he was gone, the professor prepared a swig of
his pet drink, a loathsome brew made up of bourbon,
brown sugar, and bock beer. He sipped this with relish
while reading a long article on the subject of blood. It
told him more than he wanted to know, and none of
the information promised to be of use in Black's dilemma. Until the part about sporozoan parasites. . . .

Late the next night, Middlebie, Sergeant Black, and
a small, round querulous man, known the world over as
an authority on tropical medicine, moved with the air

of conspirators up to the rear window of a certain motel apartment.

"This is the one," Black whispered.

"You're sure?" Middlebie husked in his very low monotone.

"Positive. Dell's asleep in there right now. You ready, Dr. Forrest?"

The small man said in a deep, frog-like croak, "Of course, I'm ready. But if anybody except Middlebie asked me to participate in such a fool's trick—and in the middle of the night!" His voice faded away in an irritable mutter.

Quietly, with almost surgical skill, Black made a hole in the screen. It was a warm night, and the window was up several inches. A word from Middlebie, and Forrest held something over the hole. When he removed it some moments later, the sergeant stuffed cotton into the opening. Then the three men retreated.

"Two detectives will watch the place until morning," Black said, as they got to the car. "As soon as it's light, I'll pick Dell up and, of course, I need you there too. My men can prove nobody else went into the room, but you'll have to vouch for the rest. It's going to work," he said gleefully. "It's got to!"

FROM THE TRIAL RECORD:
The State Vs.
Carleton Chambers Dell

STATE'S ATTORNEY BRAND: Please tell the court, in your own words, Professor Middlebie, just what happened on the night of June 18. Be as explicit as possible.

MIDDLEBIE: Dr. Forrest, Sergeant Black, and myself went to the Sea Foam Motel, found the rear window of the defendant's apartment, and cut a small hole in the screen. Through it, Dr. Forrest released fifty common mosquitoes, all with empty stomachs, and all dyed bright yellow with a harmless chemical pigment.

BRAND: Would you explain those points—about the empty stomachs, and the dye?

MIDDLEBIE: Certainly. Those female mosquitoes —the only kind that bite—were raised in the laboratory, in wire cages, for Dr. Forrest's work in parasitology. Consequently, any blood found in their stomachs in the morning must necessarily have come from the one warm-blooded inhabitant of that motel room. As for the dye, that insured our using only those insects released by us. That is, there was no chance of our capturing any—ah— mavericks that might have brought blood from somebody other than the defendant.

BRAND: I see. And in the morning, you did subsequently recapture some of the dyed mosquitoes?

MIDDLEBIE: Yes, from the walls of the motel room. The blood in their stomachs was typed, both by Dr. Forrest and police technicians.

BRAND: As to that, further testimony will show the blood to be of the relatively rare type spilled by the murderer in the victim's room. . . .

"I never saw a more surprised man than Dell," Black said later. "The jury was flabbergasted enough, but Dell!—I almost felt sorry for him. The jury couldn't disregard the words of men like Middlebie and Forrest. And how could *we* be blamed for the mosquitoes' 'force and violence'?"

"There's a certain subtle justice you may have overlooked," Professor Middlebie said. "Not only did Dell have a miserable night, what with fifty starved mosquitoes in that small place, but all his torture and the murder conviction—came from the females of the species."

THE ORDEAL OF RUBY MARTINSON

by Henry Slesar

I used to think that my cousin, Ruby Martinson, could do nothing more to surprise me. At the tender age of twenty-three, he had (1) committed an audacious robbery, (2) operated as a confidence man, (3) attempted burglary, and (4) plotted a series of the most ingenious crimes in the annals of the American underworld. Now, technically, Ruby never made crime pay a nickel, and the bulk of his diabolical plans never left the drawing board. But I knew, in my faint and rapidly-beating eighteen-year-old heart, that Ruby Martinson was the Evil Brain of the Century, and as his only confidante and sole possessor of his guilty secrets, I knew there was no crooked mile which Ruby wouldn't walk.

But what I never believed possible was that Ruby's granite heart would ever soften for a woman. I knew that Dorothy, his girl, exerted an uncanny influence over him, but I never suspected that it was great enough to make Ruby give up the greatest haul of his criminal career. Yet that's exactly the case, and every time I think about it, my head aches and the middle finger of my left hand throbs like a voodoo drum. You'll see why, when I tell you what happened.

It started on a day like all other days, when Ruby and I met after work in Hector's Cafeteria on Broadway. I looked forward to these meetings, to seeing Ruby's oversized head with its violent red hair, the big eyeglasses perched on his small nose, magnifying the freckles on his cheeks; to hearing Ruby blueprint some new caper, like knocking over the Chase bank, or kidnapping R. H. Macy, or swindling Merrill, Lynch, Pierce, Fenner and Smith—separately, and then en-masse. He looked particularly excited that day, but there was something peculiar about him, too. I couldn't tell what it was until I sat down, and realized that Ruby was chewing gum.

"Hey," I said. "Since when do you chew gum?"

He snickered, and kept on chewing. Then he took a pack of spearmint out of his pocket and popped another stick into his mouth. He chewed like a cow in a hurry.

"What gives, Ruby?" I said, certain that there must be method in his madness.

Still Ruby didn't answer. Then he put up his hand and removed the pink blob from his tongue. Swiftly, his hand dropped beneath the table, and came up empty. It was a pretty disgusting exhibition, and I told him so.

"That's what you think, he chuckled. "Maybe you don't know it, kid, but that little gesture's gonna make us dough."

"What little gesture?"

"That chewing gum bit. You and me are gonna clean up with the spearmint. I got the whole caper worked out."

"What caper?" I squealed. While I enjoyed taking the listener's role in Ruby's criminal plans, I continually dreaded being made an accomplice. "You're not getting *me* into another scrape," I said. "I got enough trouble. I got to find myself a job and—"

"You won't need a job," Ruby sneered. "Not for a long while." He bent forward and whispered hoarsely. "You and me are gonna knock over a jewelry store."

I gasped.

"Cut that out. We're not gonna heist it; this is something better. I've been casing this place for a week, and it's a perfect set-up. It's called Zachini's, over on Lexington Avenue."

"But, Ruby—"

"Shut up and listen. The whole thing's as easy as falling out the window. I'll do all the hard work; all you gotta do is pick up the merchandise. You see what I did with the gum?"

I nodded.

"Well, that's what I'm going to do over at Zachini's. I'm gonna walk in there, ask to see some jazzy diamond rings, and stash a hunk of spearmint under the counter."

"But why?" I said.

"Don't be a dope. That's not *all* I'm gonna stash under the counter. When the clerk's not looking, I'm gonna slip one of the rings under there, too. It'll stick to the gum. You get it now?"

I still didn't, but Ruby exhibited his usual quiet patience.

"You're the dumbest jerk in the country," he said, punching my forearm. "I'm gonna stick one of the rings under the counter and then walk out. Even if the guy notices one of the diamonds missing, he won't be able to find it on me. Then all we gotta do is go back there and pick up the haul. Get it?"

I got it now, especially about the personnel Ruby had in mind for Phase Two of his plan.

"You mean me?" I said. "But Ruby, what if they catch me?"

"Catch you? Why should they catch you? You're not doing anything. You're not even *lookin'* at rings, you dope. You're just dropping in to ask for directions or something. Meanwhile, you get your hand under that counter and—bingo!"

"No," I said, using my favorite word. "No, Ruby, I can't do that. It's too risky—"

He glared at me. "All right. So maybe you want to do the *first* job. Maybe *you* ought to start chewing gum." He shoved the spearmint package towards me, and I recoiled as if it were a loaded revolver.

"No, Ruby," I pleaded. "Not that."

"Well, it's one or the other, kid. Make up your mind."

I twisted and squirmed and argued and cajoled, but of course, it was in vain. Ruby was my Svengali, and even after several horrible experiences as his confederate in crime, I knew I didn't have the will power to resist him.

"Okay," I said finally. "I'll handle the second part."

"Good!" Ruby clapped me on the shoulder. "Then we'll meet here tomorrow, and talk it over."

"Gee, Ruby, I gotta look for a job tomorrow—"

"So look for a job! Who's stopping you? Just make sure you're at Hector's around five-thirty. That's all."

I nodded, mournfully. When Ruby offered me a stick of gum, I took it and chewed it fast, a nervous, abnormal fast.

The next day, my heart wasn't in my job-hunting. I kept thinking about Ruby, sitting at a cozy desk in some nice peaceful business office, and I wondered why he just didn't settle down and enjoy it. Ruby was an accountant, two years fresh from City College, and according to his mother, my aunt, the GREATEST accountant in the solar system. Ruby's mother was just like my mother. I mean, I was out of work just then, but my mother would tell anybody that I was the GREAT-EST unemployed person in the world. I would have given a lot for a job as good as Ruby's, but the way I felt that day, my chances were pretty slim.

But life's funny, you know? The first Help Wanted ad I answered was for a packer in a scarf company, and the fat man in charge took one look at me and said: "Okay, kiddo, you'll do." The job required no technical skill (my specialty) and it was boring but simple. I stood at a long table with four girls and an old guy, and packed whispy scarves into narrow white boxes all day long. I didn't mind the old guy, even though his breath smelled like lighter fluid, but the girls giggled all the time and made me feel like I had forgotten my pants or something.

Anyway, I met Ruby at Hector's that night, but before I could tell him about my new career, he said:

"It's all fixed, pal."

"What's fixed?"

He smiled slyly. "The jewelry caper. I went into Zachini's at noon, and had a look at their best diamond rings. Some pretty fancy rocks, all right. The clerk was a real goon; he didn't see a thing."

My eyes went so wide they began to tear.

"You mean you did it?" I gulped. "Already?"

"Sure, why waste time? First I slipped the old spearmint under the counter. Then I asked the guy to show me the stuff. The second he looked away, I had the biggest hunk of ice under the counter; he never blinked an eye."

I began to blink myself.

"N-n-now what?" I trembled.

"Are you kidding? You know what. You're going to Zachini's right now, before closing time."

"Me?" I said, in a lovely falsetto.

"Yes, you! We can't afford to waste a minute. I'll draw you a layout of the store, so you can put your hands right on the ring."

He took a napkin from the table and began doodling. I watched in fascination and horror as he made a neat blueprint of the shop, so perfectly detailed that even I couldn't mistake the location of the diamond-studded chewing gum.

I bleated some more protests, but Ruby was in no mood to be denied. It was hopeless, of course. I paid for my coffee and crullers and went out into the street, heading for the jewelry store. It was a simple enough plan. All I had to do was walk in, step up to the counter, put my hand where the gum was, remove the ring, ask the guy for some street directions, and then walk out again. At six-thirty, I was to meet Ruby at his girl's apartment.

I arrived at ten minutes to six, but it took me another five minutes to get up my nerve and open the door.

The clerk was a smooth-looking type, with hair like shoe polish. He smiled when the door jangled, but he took one look at me in my crummy sports shirt and his face changed. I said: "Can you tell me where the post office is?"

He frowned. "What do you think this is, an Esso station?"

I put my hand on the counter top and ran it along the edge until I touched something sticky.

"Gee, I'm sorry," I said. "I just thought you might know where the post office was."

"Two blocks north," he yawned, looking at his fingernails. "Turn left on Lexington."

My hand touched the metal surface of the ring. I got

it between my fingers and tugged. The gum resisted and I began to sweat.

"Boy," I said, looking through the glass-topped counter. "Sure got a bunch of nice rings there." My fingers were getting all clotted together, and for a wild moment, I was afraid I would be pinned there like a fly.

"A little expensive for you, sonny," the clerk said snootily.

Finally, the ring was in my palm. I put both my hands in my pockets and strolled towards the door.

"Thanks a lot," I said.

"You're welcome," the smoothie answered. "Next time ask a cop." I was almost glad that I was walking off with his merchandise.

I didn't glance at my prize until I was six blocks from the scene of the crime. It was a beauty, all right—a chunk of diamond the size of a small doorknob in the center, with flat slabs of diamond all around the surface of the ring. It weighed a ton, and probably cost a trillion dollars. I'd never seen anything like it.

It was too early to meet Ruby at Dorothy's house, but I was too nervous to walk the streets with the loot in my pocket. I decided to go there and wait, figuring that Dorothy wouldn't mind. That was the kind of girl Dorothy was. A real sweet type, pretty in a kind of middy-blouse way. She was a schoolteacher, and hardly the type of moll you'd expect the world's greatest criminal to have.

Just as I expected, she welcomed me cordially. We sat around the living room and chatted for a couple of minutes, and then I went into the bathroom for a close-up of the ring. Just to get a better look at it, I slipped it over the middle finger of my left hand and held it up. It flashed colored lights like a ballroom chandelier.

What a rock! I stared at it until I heard the front doorbell jangle, and knew that Ruby had arrived. Then I pulled the ring off.

That is, I tried to pull the ring off. The damned thing was stuck. I've got funny hands, with long skinny fingers and knuckles the size of pool balls. It just wouldn't budge, but I didn't get panicky or anything. I remembered how my mother used to take her wedding ring off sometimes, with soap and water. I ran some water into the sink, and lathered up. The ring still didn't move. I kept yanking at it until my finger got all red and sore.

But it didn't come off.

Well, you never saw anybody go to pieces the way I did in Dorothy's bathroom. I thrashed around the little room like a psychotic wrestler, trying to pull that lousy diamond ring off my finger. But no matter what I did, it stuck under my knuckle like it was glued there. I got so panicky that I almost bawled in frustration, but the panic didn't help. I mean, that ring was *stuck*.

Finally, not knowing what else to do, I shoved my hands into my pockets and came into the living room. Ruby was on the sofa, listening to some highbrow record Dorothy had placed on the turntable, and when I entered, he gave me a raised eyebrow in the shape of a question mark. Dorothy looked at me, too, and said:

"Why, what's the matter? You look sick!"

"I'm all right," I said weakly.

"Yeah," Ruby said icily. "What's wrong kid? Everything come off okay?"

"Not exactly," I gulped. "Could I see you in the bedroom a minute, Ruby?"

We excused ourselves and went into Dorothy's boudoir. Ruby closed the door behind us, and I told him what happened. At first, he looked relieved when he realized that the caper had been successfully completed; he didn't think there was any problem about the ring being stuck on my finger. But when he started to yank at it, I howled in pain.

"Cut it out!" he said sharply. "We'll use some soap—"

"I already tried soap," I said desperately. "Nothing works, Ruby, nothing!"

"Don't be stupid!"

We went into the bathroom, and I proved it to him. By this time, Dorothy was getting pretty curious about what was going on, and started asking questions. Rather than get her suspicious, we returned to the living room, and I kept my hands in my pockets for the rest of the visit.

Well, I hate to think about the remainder of that night. For two solid hours after we left Dorothy's, Ruby yanked and twisted and tormented the middle finger of my left hand until I was whimpering for mercy. I'd never seen Ruby so upset about anything; all his brilliant cunning seemed to desert him at the sight of that glittering rock glued to my finger. I thought sure he'd come up with some crafty scheme for getting it off, but I guess he was too overwhelmed by the whole thing. It was the biggest haul of his evil career, and it made even his great criminal intelligence totter.

Finally, Ruby gave up in disgust.

"But don't worry," he said threateningly. "We'll figure something out. And for God's sake, keep that ring out of sight!"

He didn't know what he was asking. Keeping that gleaming stone out of sight was like trying to hide a searchlight in my pocket.

I sneaked into the house that night. In bed, I kept

twisting and turning the ring in the vain hope of getting free of it. I thrashed around all night, even in my sleep, and my mother thought I was coming down with the fits for sure. I have an uncle who had a fit one night, and woke up in the morning to announce that he was going to shoot the first police horse he saw. They had to put him in some kind of home, and my mother never got over it.

When I woke up the next day, my first thought was to call up the scarf company and tell them I had a heart attack or something; the prospect of reporting to an $18-a-week job with a trillion-dollar ring on my finger was more than a little disturbing. But I knew I couldn't malinger on my second day; it would cost me the job for sure. So I put on a pair of fur-lined gloves and went to work. I know it sounds a little stupid, wearing fur-lined gloves in midsummer, but they were the only pair I owned. But when I got to the scarf company, I realized I couldn't pack those filmy things with gloves on, so I had to take them off.

For the first ten minutes, nobody noticed anything. Then the girl next to me, a black-eyed type named Maria, let out a shriek.

"Looka him! Ain't that *adorable?*" She covered her mouth and started to gasp and giggle at the same time.

"Cut it out," I growled.

"Isn't that *sweet?*" another girl said. "He musta gotten engaged."

"Ain't that nice," Maria said. "We'll have to give him a shower, huh, girls?"

Luckily, the fat guy who ran the place came over and wanted to know what all the squealing was about. He looked at me funny when they told him, and backed away like I had some kind of disease or something.

The rest of the day was awful; I never heard so much giggling in my life. It was like working in a tickle factory.

That evening, I met Ruby at Hector's and said:

"You gotta do something, Ruby! I can't go on like this!"

"Shut up!" he said angrily. "It's all your fault, you dope. We'll just have to figure something out."

"Look, can't we file it off?"

"We can't take the chance of ruining it. It's got all those baguettes around it; it'll take an expert to file it off, and experts ask too many questions. You'll just have to wear it until I think of an answer."

"But, Ruby—"

"I said shut up!" Ruby said, and I knew he meant it.

I went home early and stayed in my room. About eight-thirty, the telephone rang and it was Ruby. He wanted me to meet him at the corner of 43rd Street and Seventh Avenue, and I hurried over there, hopeful that his great brain had at last arrived at a solution. I was to be disappointed, however. There was somebody else with Ruby, a seedy-looking old guy with a greasy felt hat. Despite the warm weather, he wore a windbreaker with patches on the elbows. To tell you the truth, he looked like a bum.

Ruby said: "This is Mr. Feener. He's in the diamond business."

Mr. Feener shifted his feet uncomfortably, and looked up and down the street. "Okay, okay, let's go. I ain't got all night."

"Show him," Ruby said, and yanked my left hand out of my pocket.

Mr. Feener took one look at the ring, and then hauled me towards the street light. It was very undignified. He put a jeweler's loop in his eye and started his examination. I felt pretty silly, let me tell you. Then the old bum muttered:

"Not bad, not bad. Nice blue-white specimen. Not bad at all."

"How much?" Ruby said, licking his lips.

"Well, I dunno. I think maybe I could manage fifteen hundred." His eyes went crafty. "Who knows? Maybe even two grand, if I talked to the right people. But that's my top price."

"No dice," Ruby said. "You'll have to do better than that."

Mr. Feener yanked my finger to his eyes again, ignoring my yelp of indignation.

"Twenty-five hundred tops," he said. "That's my final offer."

"Make it three," Ruby said.

"Twenty-seven," Feener said.

"Twenty-eight."

"It's a deal," the old guy sighed. "Only you'll have to get the ring off his hand. I can't sell the kid, too."

Ruby was practically hopping up and down with excitement by this time, and I was a little bug-eyed myself. Twenty-eight hundred dollars! It was a fortune. It was practically Ruby's yearly salary.

Then Ruby drew Mr. Feener aside, and they went into a huddle. All of a sudden, I began to get scared. I had been merely annoyed until then, having to submit my finger to Mr. Feener's inspection, but now I was scared. What if there *wasn't* any way to file the ring off? After all, weren't diamonds the hardest substance known to man? What if Ruby was going to do something *really* drastic?

They came out of the conference, and I heard Ruby say:

"Okay, then. We'll just have to cut it off."

That was all I needed to hear. I started to shake like a palsied marionette, and took off down that street like the devil was after me. I think I would have preferred the devil; the idea of Ruby Martinson chasing me, with his horrible evil mind fixed on that twenty-eight hundred dollars, was far more terrifying. I think I broke the four-minute mile making my getaway, and I didn't stop running until I thought I was going to drop dead.

Then I started to think. I couldn't go home—Ruby would be sure to find me there. There was only one sensible course, and that was to throw myself on the mercy of Dorothy, Ruby's girl. She was the only one I knew who might have the power to temper Ruby's evil determination.

Dorothy was practicing on the piano when I arrived, and she looked surprised to see me. One look at my face must have told her I was in trouble, and she started asking questions.

"You've got to help me," I stammered. "It's Ruby—"

"Ruby? Is he in trouble?"

"No! It's me that's in trouble. Look—"

I pulled my hand out of my pocket and showed her the ring. She backed off as if temporarily blinded, and then came closer. At first her face was blank, and then she giggled suddenly.

"Why, it's lovely," she said, stifling a smile. "But don't you think it's a little—well I mean, a boy your age—"

"It's not *my* ring," I said hastily. "It's Ruby's. It got stuck on my finger and I can't get it off. No matter what I do."

"Oh," she said, examining it again. "It *is* beautiful. And you say . . . Ruby bought it?" She started playing with the curls on the back of her head.

"Yes," I said miserably. "Ruby bought it. But now

he's going to cut my finger off."

"He's *what?*"

"I *know* he is, Dorothy. I heard him say!"

"Oh, that's silly! Ruby would never do such a thing."

"You don't know him," I said gloomily, for a moment tempted to spill the whole story of Ruby's ghastly secret life. "He'll do *anything* to get this ring. It means a lot to him."

"It does?" Dorothy said coyly, twisting my hand around to get a good look at it. "Why should an engagement ring be so important to Ruby?"

"A what?" I said blankly.

"It's certainly lovely," Dorothy crooned, her eyes going all mushy. "It's the loveliest engagement ring I ever saw."

"But, Dorothy—"

"And you really can't *blame* Ruby for being upset. It's not every day that he buys an engagement ring, is it? But don't worry about getting it off. Come on with me."

She took me by the hand and led me into the kitchen. Then she opened the refrigerator door, and stuck my hand into the freezer compartment.

"You just stay there a minute," she said, "and I'll be right back. Don't move."

I did what she said, feeling like an idiot. When she returned, there was a jar of vaseline in her hand.

"It's the warm weather," she explained. "It makes your finger swell. So first we freeze it, and then we use a little of this."

She took my hand out of the freezer; by this time my finger was a beautiful shade of blue. Then she smeared the gooey stuff all over it, and the ring slid off, slick as grease.

I breathed a sigh of relief, and rubbed my aching

digit. But then I saw Dorothy slip the ring onto her own finger, and shouted: "Don't, Dorothy!"

"Oh, it's all right," she said. "I just wanted to get used to the feel of it."

"Could—could I have the ring please, Dorothy?"

"I'll return it to Ruby. Don't worry about it."

"But Dorothy—"

"I said don't worry about it," Dorothy said, in a voice colder than the freezer. Then she turned away from me.

There was nothing else I could do except go to the door and leave. She didn't even hear me say good-bye.

I didn't see Ruby until the next day. I walked into Hector's, and there he was at his usual table, but there was something about his expression that was definitely unusual.

"Hi, Ruby," I said timidly.

He didn't answer. He looked straight ahead, sipping coffee.

"Gee, Ruby, I'm sorry about last night—"

"Forget it," he said curtly.

"Did you see Dorothy? Did you get the ring back?"

"Yeah, I got it."

"Gee, that's good," I sighed. "I was worried there for awhile. Did you get the money from Feener?"

"No. I gave the damn thing back."

"You *what?*"

"I put the ring in a package and mailed it back to Zachini's."

"Gave it back?" I repeated stupidly. "But why, Ruby?"

He turned on me savagely.

"Because I couldn't give Dorothy a hot ring, that's why. I couldn't get my girl into a jam, could I?"

"No, I guess not."

He sat silently for a full minute, and then he pulled out a velvet box.

"What's that, Ruby?"

He flipped it open. There was another ring inside. It had only one diamond, and it was no bigger than a bee-bee shot. It was sort of cute, but nothing like the first ring.

"You took *another* one?" I said.

"No," Ruby growled. "I bought it."

"Bought it?"

"For Dorothy. We—we got engaged last night."

"Engaged?"

"Yeah. Don't ask me how it happened. When I went up to see her, she threw her arms around me and—aw, what's the difference." He looked moodily at the shiny beebee-shot ring. "It was Dorothy's idea that I return the other ring. She said we couldn't afford a ring like that. She said we ought to put the money into the bank or something . . ." He snapped the box closed. "Anyway, that's what I did."

"Gee, Ruby," I said, overcome by the depth of the tragedy. "I'm sorry. I mean—congratulations."

He muttered something under his breath, but I couldn't hear it. Of course, I knew what had happened was all my fault. I sure hoped Ruby wouldn't hold it against me. After all, there are a lot better enemies you can have in this world than the Greatest Criminal Brain of the Century.

GARCIA'S BULLS

by Hal Ellson

The Hacienda stood in open desert country some twenty miles outside the city of Montes. An immense ruin, it was tenantless but for a caretaker and a few hands to watch over Pedro Garcia's bulls, which were very special. All were black, huge, mean, notable for their courage, and bred to fight. In the Plaza de Toros on the dusty outskirts of Montes, no other bulls were acceptable and a corrida without them was unthinkable. Just as unthinkable was the idea of anyone making off with one of these wild brutes—and yet five of them had vanished without trace.

Did they wander off into the empty desert? No, the barbed-wire fences were intact. Nor had they been cut and rejoined, indicating that the bulls had been taken through the gate, which bespoke nerve to a high degree, considering the chance the thief took of running into Señor Garcia, a giant of a man with a temper that matched his size.

But who, in the first place, would be foolish enough to make off with the bulls, much less risk a chance meeting with their owner? This, exactly, was the question Detective Victor Fiala put to Chief Lopez in his office. A reasonable question, but Lopez, a not altogether reasonable person, said, "That's for you to figure out, Victor."

"I just hope this isn't a joke," answered Fiala.

"Hardly," said Lopez. "Garcia's sworn to get the thief and you know what that means."

"I know, but why would anyone steal the bulls?"

This from Fiala, who should know better? Lopez smiled. "Thieves are thieves, aren't they?" he allowed. "One will steal from a poor box, another, given the chance, will abstract your eyeballs. In other words, a thief will steal anything, as you are fond of saying."

"Anything within reason," Fiala put in.

"Five prize bulls. Isn't that within reason, Victor?"

"Yes and no. The thief can't sell them for the ring with Garcia's brand on them. Nobody'd touch them."

"Admitted," said Lopez, "but someone made off with them, and that's the point."

Fiala shook his head. "Blooded bulls. Any one of them good for breeding, but where could one hide five of them? Those brutes need plenty of room on an open range." The old detective shook his head again. "I'm afraid the thief doesn't intend to breed them."

"Which leads us to what?"

"They may have been butchered."

"What I was thinking," said Lopez.

"May have been," Fiala said, "but I doubt it."

"And what causes you to doubt they were butchered? They'd make a lot of steak."

"Tough steak, for one thing, Señor, but my doubt stems from another source. I can't imagine anyone but a madman slaughtering a Garcia bull."

"Hm," said Lopez, his eyes lighting up. "That may well be your lead."

"My lead?"

"A madman. That's the answer to this mess. No one else would commit such an act."

Fiala frowned, weighed the theory and found it

wanting. The butchering might occur to a madman, but how would such a person, with a mind so disjointed, be able to plan, organize and carry out the abduction of five intractable bulls, each capable of killing a man with a flick of a horn? This he explained, but Lopez wouldn't have it.

"The fellow has to be mad," he insisted. "No citizen in his right mind would ever dream of such an act. But enough of talk, Victor. Garcia wants action, and so do I. There's the door. Get on your burro and go to work."

There was no burro, of course. Fiala's car awaited him outside headquarters. A small moon-faced boy in bare feet stood beside it. "Clean your windshield?" he greeted the detective.

"Clean it, but no spit on the rag," Fiala answered and walked on, crossing the blistering plaza to the Blue Moon Restaurant. Coffee was in order, black and bitter to stir his brain. He ordered, and the counterman served him.

"What about Garcia's bulls?" that one said.

"What about them?"

"A sacrilege to steal them, no?"

"A mortal sin, at least."

"Are you working on the case?"

"I am."

"Any leads?"

"None as yet." Fiala drank half his coffee and asked, "What kind of person do you think would steal Garcia's bulls?"

The counterman splayed his hands, arched his brows and said, "Only a crazy man."

Another Lopez. Fiala finished his coffee, left and crossed the plaza to his car. The boy had cleaned the windshield and was waiting for his pay. Fiala handed him a peso and drove to the Black Cat. The cantina was empty, Pancho enjoying a small beer behind the bar.

"Any news on the bulls?" he asked as Fiala stepped through the side door.

"Too early yet. Let me have a small one. It's hot out there."

Pancho opened a bottle and shook his bald head. "Bad, bad," he sighed. "What kind of bullfights will we see if Garcia's stock is stolen?"

"They may as well close the arena and throw the key away. What's to be done? The thief will have to be caught, but . . ."

"That's easier said than done." Pancho wiped his bald head. "I don't envy you, Victor, especially on this one."

"Meaning what?"

"Anyone who'd dare steal those bulls would be a dangerous person to deal with. You'll have to watch your step."

"So you think the thief is—"

"A killer. What else could he be?" Pancho lifted his beer. "Here's luck, and take care."

The rustler a killer? An unpleasant thought. Fiala finished his drink and left. The sun was hotter now, not a breath of air stirring. He drove off, turned into a wide and empty highway sentineled by two columns of enormous royal palms. This causeway led directly into the desert that encroached on the northern sector of the city and here the sun fired a white and dusty landscape when nothing moved.

A mile outside the city he swung off the highway and followed a winding road that had been pounded into definition by the hooves of burros and heavy-wheeled oxcarts. An alkali-white trail to nowhere, but finally a squat ranch house surrounded by ancient walls appeared in the distance. Cattle resting in the shade of the trees lifted their heads as the car drew close. A rough mesquite fence encircled the house. Fiala braked at the gate, stepped from the car, and a tall, broad-shouldered man came from the ranch house, a holstered pistol on his right hip, a white Texan hat angled on his head.

Fiala went through the gate, and Señor Garcia greeted and invited him inside where he opened two bottles of beer. They saluted, drank and got down to business. Did Garcia have any idea how his bulls had been stolen?

"I've no idea," said Garcia, "but the thief's taken the last." He slapped his holster. "I'm staying at the Hacienda from tonight on."

"You're angry and I can't blame you," said Fiala, "but bullets won't settle the matter."

"You think not?"

"I know. Kill someone and you're in trouble."

"Not if there are no witnesses and no body."

"Meaning what? You'll bury the fellow in the desert?" Fiala shrugged. "Bodies have a way of showing up and the dead have a way of talking, but that's beside the point. I don't want to go after you, but if I must I will. Meantime let me track down the thief."

"Thanks, but I didn't send for you.

"I know, but Lopez gave me the assignment. I didn't ask for it."

"I appreciate the favor; the help I don't need."

Fiala grinned to himself, knowing Garcia well. A good fellow, but a hothead who would certainly do as he said and damn himself in the bargain. *Stop him, but how?* He shook his head. "This is going to be difficult enough," he said, "and now you're complicating things."

"If I settle the matter myself?"

"Exactly. You're doubling my load, and I'm getting a

little too old for that sort of thing."

"Ah, you're asking for sympathy."

"No, simply stating the truth. I'd like your cooperation."

"No promises, Victor," Garcia said, relenting a bit. "I'll try not to use the gun, but I'll be waiting at the gate to the Hacienda tonight."

"You didn't have a man there?"

"I did, but he could have been bought off."

Fiala shook his head. "I doubt if he'd take the chance, and doubly I doubt that the bulls passed through the gate."

"The fence wasn't cut. My men went over every inch of it."

Nodding, Fiala let that pass and said, "I'm going to the Hacienda and look around. Care to go along?"

"A waste of time, but . . ."

A long drive deeper into the desert brought them to the Hacienda which stood a quarter-mile back from the road in an area below the desert floor. From the road itself there was no sign of the Hacienda. A hundred yards past the gate it came into view, a massive white ruin which had been built during the Conquest. As the car stopped in front of it, Fiala shook his head, as impressed as on those other occasions when he'd seen it. "Beautiful and sad," he remarked. "Three hundred years of history coming to an end."

"Everything ends," Garcia shrugged.

"Have you been inside?"

"Only in the chapel. The other rooms are too dangerous to chance."

"What about the corral?"

"Nothing's there."

Nothing? Fiala smiled to himself. Garcia, he realized, had rented the land surrounding it for his bulls and the Hacienda itself didn't concern him in the least. "A lot of history here," the detective remarked. "One wonders how the Spaniards found this spot. They must have been a very tough and remarkable breed of men."

"I suppose they were," Garcia conceded.

"They were quite resourceful. They found water here and built the Hacienda around it."

"Around it? The stream is over there, outside the walls."

"True," said Fiala. "But it goes underground inside the corral."

"I know of the well, not of the underground stream."

"It's there, all right."

"If you say so," Garcia answered. "Now, let's get down to business. Do you want to question my men? Not that it will do much good. They don't know anything."

"In that case, there's no point in speaking to them."

"And no point in coming here."

Fiala shrugged. "The ride was pleasant, and this place." He nodded toward the Hacienda. "Beautiful and sad. If you don't mind, I'd like to walk around it."

"As you wish, but don't be long, and take care. You don't know what may topple on your head."

Fiala laughed and walked off, following the south wall. Gaping cracks and mounds of debris testified to the pillage of time. *Sad. Sad.* He shook his head, moved on, came to an opening in the wall and stepped through; worm-eaten rafters, a huge hole in the ceiling, rubble on the dirt floor of a muted room . . . *Is it safe to cross?* Quickly he passed through it and entered the corral, an open area within the walls and stark empty but for what appeared to be a squat hut at its center. For some moments he surveyed the corral, then approached the squat structure, stopped and examined the ground before it.

Some minutes later, he returned to the car, found Garcia dozing in the front seat and climbed behind the wheel. "Ah, so you're back, Victor," Garcia said, opening his eyes. "Find anything?"

Fiala shrugged, started the car, drove to the road, then on to the ranch house. Garcia climbed out. "Back where we started and nothing accomplished," he said.

"A point of view, Señor."

"You mean you found something at the Hacienda?"

"Perhaps, but I'd rather not discuss it just now. Meantime, have I your word that you won't use your pistol?"

Garcia smiled. "Let's say I won't shoot the thief if I catch up with him, but I may tap him on the head."

"Then you're going to lay for him?"

"At the gate to the Hacienda."

"A waste of time. Your bulls weren't taken through it."

"You sound sure of that, but how do you know?"

"Let's say I have a hunch, shall we? And now I'm off to gather a little information. Adios, Señor."

The ride back across the desert was uneventful. Fiala was in no hurry and was rather pleased with the way things were going. For one, he was certain he knew how the bulls had been taken from the Hacienda. A guess on his part plus his visit there had convinced him, but this, if he were correct, was the easy part. The question that bothered him now? Who was the thief, and how had he disposed of the bulls? If a killer were involved, then violence no doubt would ensue.

If only I were ten years younger, he thought, doubting his chances of outshooting the rustler in an encounter with guns. Now the car moved out of the desert and speared at the shadows cast by giant palms; shadows but no people, the sun blistering Montes, the city silent and dozing; a day unfit for a dog. The car rolled into the plaza behind headquarters, braked at the Blue Moon Restaurant.

Fiala got out. As expected, the Blue Moon was empty. *Not even a fly to nag one,* he thought, and stepped outside. A man in a black suit and turned-around collar was coming toward him, his face gaunt and waxen— Padre Mendoza, whose way was different, to say the least. An odd one, his chief concern was the army of ragged, barefooted shoe-shine boys who worked the plazas; that was his flock.

"Padre." Fiala bowed his head.

The priest stopped. His dark eyes flashed as if fire smoldered in their depths. "Victor, you haven't forgotten the contribution?"

"No, but it will take a little time collecting the money. Pay day should do it."

"The best time, before the money goes on foolishness. Forgive me for speaking like this, but my boys are always in need. You understand?"

"Of course."

"But most of the others don't. All the money goes to Boys Town. The kids there have everything, and mine have nothing."

True. Those of wealth and importance in Montes supported Boys Town, but for the padre's ragged army, nothing. Fiala nodded in sympathy. *The padre's cause is a better one, but the man himself? A fanatic who doesn't get off one's back till he gets what he wants for his boys. And what he wants now is a school.*

He mentioned this to Fiala and said, "The money you collect from your co-workers will go toward that."

"A school?" said Fiala. "The money you get from us will never cover it."

"Ah, but I already have the building, an abandoned schoolhouse across the riverbed. The mayor's wife used her influence on her husband, so . . ." The padre shrugged. "A little paint, some nails for the broken benches, glass for the windows and . . ."

"And the teacher?"

"Myself. Classes will be at night when the little fellows finish shining shoes and after they've eaten. A full belly first. Isn't that right?" The padre laughed and his eyes flashed. He was a man with a mission, and now he had to run. Someone had promised a donation of pencils and paper for the school. "I expect to see you pay day," he said, and hurried off as if the Devil were at his heels.

And in this heat, thought Fiala, nodding and turning to the gutter. He crossed it and entered the plaza. On one of the paths an ancient sour-orange tree shadowed a bench. He sat, lit a cigarette and thought of the padre flying to his mission. *A nice fellow, but a bit of a dreamer.* He sighed. *A bit? More than that. Much more. What had he said about a school for the shoe-shine boys?* "Ridiculous," he mumbled and looked about.

Five minutes later he drove up to the Black Cat, and entered the cantina by the side door.

"Back?" said Pancho from behind the bar.

"Back."

"Anything new?"

"Nothing. I'll have a double tequila."

Pancho arched his brows, filled the glass and watched its contents vanish as if it were water.

"Many thanks. I needed that," Fiala said and out he went as fast as he'd come.

Tequila in his blood and a wild thought in his brain, off he drove through the dozing streets. A five-minute run and he turned into the city's main plaza and there, as if on a carrousel, twice he rounded it before he made up his mind to go where he did not want to go.

A short drive brought him to a bridge spanning a dry riverbed. Abruptly beyond the bridge, the streets rose sharply, pavement vanished, replaced by mud and pot-holes. Upward the car climbed, a rough going and a passage through an area of crumbling adobes and rickety shacks. High up on the mountain slope a white stucco structure stood by itself, a forlorn sight, without windows and its massive door hanging precariously on a single hinge—Padre Mendoza's school.

Fiala braked the car, got out, stared at the forlorn structure and shook his head. He went to the door, looked inside. Nothing but rubble. Turning away, he gazed at a cluster of decrepit shacks standing thirty yards away. One, larger than the rest, served as a gathering place for the padre's shoe-shine boys and it was here that he served them meals, taught them the fear of God and housed those who were homeless. Siding the shack and topped by broken glass stood a crude wall which formed a small corral. Fiala turned from it, changed his mind and approached the wall. Six feet of adobe confronted him, topped with glittering fragments of glass. *Is the other side worth a look?* He reached up carefully, gripped the wall, pulled himself up, looked, then dropped back to the ground.

A creaking of wheels and slow clopping of hooves brought him about. Coming toward him was an oxcart with two men aboard, one a grizzled old fellow wearing a sombrero, the other Padre Mendoza. The cart came abreast of Fiala and halted. The padre jumped down, his eyes flashing. "Ah, you came to see my school?"

"No, Padre."

"Then you brought a contribution?"

"No, Padre."

"Then why?" The padre stopped. His eyes flashed
fire, he seemed about to lunge at the detective, caught
himself and began to tremble violently. The trembling
ceased abruptly and he stiffened, his eyes flashed again.
He looked like a trapped and wounded animal ready
to fight to the last.

Fiala felt sorry for him, sorry for the shoe-shine boys
that no one cared about. *Who will shelter the homeless
ones and feed the hungry?*

"Garcia's bulls." The words hissed through the
padre's clenched teeth. "That's why you're here."

Fiala nodded. "I'm sorry, Padre. You were the last
person I suspected. I didn't want to believe it, but
certain conclusions forced me to."

"And what do you expect to charge me with?" The
padre was bristling now.

"You know what the charge will be."

The padre shook his head and sent Fiala a glacial
smile. "That I made off with Señor Garcia's bulls? No,
Victor."

"You deny the charge?"

"Let us say that I took from the rich to give to the
poor, and would one define that as stealing? To give is
sacred, is it not?"

From the moment he'd got into this business, Fiala
had anticipated an awkward scene such as this was
shaping into, and now he felt embarrassed, for the law
was the law, and yet the padre had a point. He admitted
to this, and the padre said, "Besides, Señor Garcia is
very wealthy. He can well afford those bulls."

"No doubt, but who gave you the right—"

"To give another man's property away?" The padre

smiled again, his eyes blazed wildly. A saint bent on martyrdom or a fanatic moved by compulsions he did not understand might have looked as he did. "God gave me the right," he said, striking his chest.

Is he invoking the Creator as a shield, or does he truly believe this? But more to the point, would God grant anyone the right to steal? Fiala put that to him, thinking he'd stop the padre. It didn't work.

"To the needy He granted me the right to give," the padre answered. "And I did just that."

"And slaughtered five bulls."

"With more mercy than they'd ever receive in the arena. They died for a good cause, not to the stupid applause of the *aficionados* of death."

"That is a lot of meat."

"Yes, instead of tortillas and beans, plenty of steak for my boys, and what they couldn't put away, you saw when you looked over the wall."

Fiala nodded. Beyond the wall jerked beef drying in the sun and blackened with legions of flies; evidence to doom the padre.

The padre smiled. "Do you still charge me?" he asked. "Or do you acknowledge that God's law transcends man's?"

Fiala shrugged. "For the record," he said, "perhaps we can say the bulls were taken by an unknown party and are not recoverable."

The padre smiled, his manner changed, eyes softened. "Concerning the brutes," he said, "how did you know I was the one?"

"A combination of things and a process of elimination, Padre, but most of all yourself when we met earlier and you spoke of your school and the boys. 'Full bellies first,' that was the phrase you used. It stuck in my mind."

"Gave myself away. Ah, I should have known better."

"It happens to the best of us." Fiala shrugged. "And now I must leave to unravel some complications with Chief Lopez. Also, Señor Garcia will have to be placated, and you can help, Padre, if you'll give your word that you won't go near the Hacienda again."

"But . . ."

"No buts. Garcia's staying at the Hacienda and wearing a gun which he intends to use. Now, what of the shoe-shine boys? Who'll feed and care for them if something happens to you?"

The padre, hearing the threat to his boys, conceded, and Fiala drove off.

Back to headquarters he went, confronted Lopez and dropped the bomb: Padre Mendoza was the one who'd made off with Garcia's bulls, but he hadn't arrested him, pointing out that to throw him in the lockup wouldn't do, for the people of Montes, without doubt, would storm the jail and carry the padre out like a martyred saint.

Lopez saw the point, but a fly was in the ointment: how to explain the business to Garcia?

"Difficult, but if one took the bull by the horns, it could be managed," Fiala answered, and out the door he went.

Again he rode into the desert. Night caught him and on went his headlights. A half hour later, his spotlight snared a wire fence, but where was the gate in this wilderness of night? Two tall yuccas alerted him. He hit the brake, stepped from the car and a blow toppled him, a flashlight beamed in his face. Garcia stood over him. "Are you hurt, Victor?"

"Down but not out. Give me a hand."

Garcia pulled him to his feet and shook his head.

"Too bad. I thought I had the raider."

"He's been caught. His name? Padre Mendoza," Fiala said, and quickly explained why he hadn't arrested the priest.

Garcia digested this slowly, then suddenly burst out laughing. "The man's mad," he declared, "and you were right for not arresting him. But tell me, how did he get away with my bulls?"

Fiala smiled. "Perhaps you'll recall the underground stream I mentioned in the center of the corral? Well, that's not all that's there. Just beyond the stream, the Spaniards dug a passage that leads out to the road. If the Hacienda fell to an attack—but that's ancient history. You want to know how the padre managed to control the brutes and how he got them out to the road. Simple. He had an oxcart standing by and a helper, the old fellow who handles the bulls when they arrive at the arena. He and the padre unhitched the oxen, took them through the passage and brought them back with a bull between them, somewhat the way they do when they bring the brutes into the arena-corral the day before the fight. The oxen quiet the bulls, as you well know."

"I know, but how did they get the bulls on the cart?" Garcia asked.

"Simpler yet. They had a cow aboard the cart and a ramp for the convenience of the bulls. Of course, they abducted only one bull at a time, so they must have worked all night."

"Clever," Garcia said, "but how did my men miss the action?"

"Simple again," Fiala explained. "Like you, they didn't know about the underground passage and, like everyone else, they never expected anyone would dare steal the bulls."

Garcia digested that and laughed. "Know what I think?" he said. "The padre isn't as mad as one might believe."

"Correct," said Fiala, turning to his car. "Drive you back to the ranch, Señor?"

THE MIDNIGHT TRAIN
by John Lutz

From far in front of Ulman the shrill, drawn out sound of the locomotive's whistle drifted back, long and lonely notes, like the forlorn wails of a distant siren. Ulman, bracing himself against a rough plywood wall, in the swaying boxcar, rose slowly. He could feel the train losing speed already as it slowed for the unmarked and seldom used crossing just outside of Erebville. It wouldn't do for him to ride all the way into the Erebville switchyard, for he'd been told that the railroad dicks were tough and eager there, especially this time of year, when the hoboes and migrant fruit pickers were moving west. Ulman had been told back east by a knowledgeable one-eyed hobo that the train would slow for this crossing about midnight, and that was the time to leap.

He made his way across the lurching car to the wide steel door that was closed all the way to a warped two-by-four, which he'd jammed in place to keep from getting locked in. He held on to the edge of the door for a moment, drew a deep breath, then with all his strength shot it sliding open.

Cool country air rushed in on him as he looked out into moonless darkness. He rubbed his grizzled chin, waiting for just the right moment. As the train rolled to its slowest point, then began to regain its speed, he leaped.

Ulman got to his feet slowly, slapping the dust off his clothes. His legs felt rubbery after the constant motion and his ears missed the constant roar. He grinned as the roar diminished and he saw the train's lights disappear in the distance. Tomorrow he'd hike to the other side of Erebville and jump the next twelve o'clock train west.

But where to spend the night? That was the problem, but a problem that Ulman had solved hundreds of times before. He stared about him into the darkness, and then he saw the lights. They appeared to be coming from the window of a house about a mile off. It struck Ulman as odd that one of these country families would be up so late, and lucky, for he might be able to negotiate for a bunk in an outbuilding. If not that, at least he'd have a chance for a good feed in the morning. He made sure that nothing had fallen from his pockets, then set off walking.

It turned out to be a small frame farmhouse, and the only outbuildings were a ramshackle barn and a pigpen, neither of which appealed to Ulman as night quarters. He walked quietly toward the porch, noting that the usually present farm dog hadn't barked to reveal his presence. Before stepping up on the porch he decided to peek in one of the shadeless windows.

The inside of the house was dirty and cheaply furnished. The naked bulb in the ceiling fixture cast bright light over a worn carpet, ancient, ready-to-collapse chairs and a ripped sofa. Ulman decided to sleep in the open tonight and approach the house again in the morning for breakfast. He was about to turn away when a woman entered the room.

Her inexpensive flower-print dress matched her surroundings, but the woman didn't. She was about thirty, Ulman guessed, tall and graceful, with fine features, straight brown hair and very large blue eyes. Though the dress she wore was obviously cheap, it couldn't have been designed or worn better to show off her curvaceous figure. The hemline was well above shapely knees, the waist drawn in, the neckline low. She held a white cat cradled in her left arm while she idly stroked it with a graceful right hand. Ulman could tell somehow by her actions that she was alone.

Her beauty caused Ulman to draw in his breath sharply. The remoteness of the situation sent very evil thoughts darting across his mind, thoughts which he quickly dispelled, for Ulman was a poetic if not a literate man, a man who appreciated beauty and was at the same time bound by the peculiar morality of his type.

As he watched, the woman set the cat down and smoothed her dress sensually, seductively, with her slender hands. Ulman backed away from the window, frightened by the lust that was pounding through his veins, knowing to what it could ultimately lead. He turned and made himself walk quietly away. Then he made himself run.

Just after sunrise the next morning, Ulman rose from his cramped position beneath a tree, stretched, brushed off his canvas windbreaker, and began walking toward the farmhouse.

The house appeared more squalid in the daylight than it had the night before. Ulman noted that the fields surrounding it were grown over with weeds. He saw no stock except for a hog near the barn and several chickens in the barren farmyard. Then he noted two more hogs on the other side of the barn, but his eyes were trained on them for only a second. They switched immediately to the woman, still wearing the print dress, hanging a breeze-whipped line of wash.

She was aware of him, Ulman could tell, but she pretended not to notice him as she stretched upward to fasten clothespins as he approached. He stood silently for a moment, taking her in with his eyes, aware of the sharp, scrunching sound of wood and rope on wet cloth as she jammed down the final clothespin to hold a sheet to the line, then turned. There was no surprise or fear in her blue eyes, and this made Ulman even more ill at ease in the face of her beauty.

"Your mister at home?" he asked. He knew the answer to that.

"Ain't no mister here," she said, shifting her weight to one foot and staring frankly at him.

"I, uh, wonder," Ulman said, "if you could spare a bite of breakfast. I'd be willin' to work for it."

She ignored the question. "You hopped off'n that freight went by here last night, didn't you?"

Ulman's heart leaped. Had she seen him at the window? He decided to play it casually. "Sure did, missy. On my way to a job in California."

"California's a long ways."

"Sure is." Ulman rubbed his chin. "How'd you know I come off that freight?"

"Lots of fellas do," she said. "For some reason they don't want to ride all the way in to Erebville."

"Railroad dicks," Ulman said bitterly. "Always ready to lay a club alongside a man's head."

The woman smiled suddenly. "My name's Cyrila."

Ulman returned the grin, ashamed of his soiled clothes and dirty face. "Lou Ulman."

"Well, Mr. Ulman, you can wash up there at the pump an' I'll fix us some eggs."

Ulman grinned again, his eyes involuntarily running

up and down the woman. "I appreciate it, ma'am."

Surprisingly the breakfast of scrambled eggs, bread, fresh-brewed coffee, and a tall glass of orange juice looked delicious. Ulman sat down across from the woman at the table and began to eat with enthusiasm as he discovered the food to be as tasty as it looked. After the first few bites he realized she was staring at him.

"You say you live here alone?" he asked, wiping a corner of his mouth with a forefinger.

Cyrila nodded, her blue eyes still fixed on him intently. "Husband died five years ago."

Ulman took a large bite of bread and talked around it. "Quite a job makin' ends meet for a woman, ain't it? What do you raise?"

"Pigs, mostly. A few chickens."

Ulman nodded. "Them's nice lookin' pigs. How many you got?"

The woman sipped her coffee. " 'Bout a dozen. Hard to keep more'n that in feed. I sell 'em in the fall when they're fat enough and use some of the money to buy piglets."

"Start all over again then, huh?"

The woman nodded, smiling her beautiful smile. "Toilin' in the fields ain't woman's work," she said with a hint of coyness. "Pigs is about all that's left in these parts. Good profit in 'em if you can afford to feed 'em all summer long."

Ulman finished his eggs and licked the fork appreciatively.

"More, Mr. Ulman?" Her eyelids fluttered exaggeratedly and he suspected she was trying to use her feminine wiles on him, trying to lead him on.

He thought, looking at her, *I ain't that lucky.* "No, no thank you, ma'am. I'm full up."

"If you will, call me Cyrila," she said, toying with her coffee spoon.

Ulman hesitated, then smiled. "Sure will," he said, "Cyrila."

"There's a stack of firewood out behind the barn," she said smiling. "It does need—"

"Now, Cyrila," Ulman interrupted, "I said I'd work for my food an' I meant it. Just show me where the ax is."

After he'd chopped wood for an hour, Ulman found himself scything down the tall weeds behind the house, then mending the crude wire fence that surrounded the pigpen on the other side of the barn. Most of the time he worked he sang to himself, all the time watching for Cyrila as she worked in the house and yard. Now and then she'd smile and wave to him from a window, or turn from getting water at the pump and give him a warm look.

It must get lonely out here without a man, Ulman muttered, wielding the heavy hammer. It must.

It was almost sundown when he finished. He washed up at the pump while she stood gracefully on the porch, watching. He let the still-hot sun dry him briefly, slipped on his shirt, slicked back his hair with wet fingers and walked toward her, following her into the house.

It was cooler inside the house, and dim. The reverberating slam of the rusty screen door rang through the heavy air and left them in silence.

"You surely did a good day's work," she said. Her smile seemed a little forced this time, and she held onto the back of the old sofa as if for support.

He grinned and shrugged. "I guess you need a man around here, is all."

"Don' I know it, now?" She stepped away from the

sofa. "I bet you sure worked up a thirst."

"Thirst? Well, yeah. It's close to that ol' bewitchin' hour, though, an' I gotta be on the other side of Erebville to jump that train. But if you got somethin' around . . ."

"I think there's some still in the cupboard," she said, the smile still set on her face. "It'll be old. Jus' use it for guests and medicine."

Ulman followed her into the kitchen. "The older the better."

His eyes roved up her as she stood on her toes to reach the top shelf. There were some cans and three bottles up there, two off-brand whiskeys and a more expensive bourbon bottle half full. She got down the expensive bottle and turned, handing it to him.

Ulman took a long swig, savoring the smoothness and warmth of the bourbon. The woman was watching him. He moved to hand the bottle back to her and her hand closed on his, squeezing the fingers around the neck of the bottle as if she meant for him to keep it. He was surprised to see that she was on the verge of crying.

"You're right, Mr. Ulman," she said, looking up at him. "I surely do need a man around here." She buried her head on his shoulder, sobbing, her body pressed against him. With his right hand Ulman held the bottle, with his left Cyrila's warm back. With his foot he kicked open the bedroom door.

It was pitch dark in the farmhouse when Cyrila rose. She stood by the bed, stretching languidly, then walked barefoot into the kitchen. She placed the bourbon bottle back in the cupboard, aside from the other bottles, and slipped into some old coveralls, rolled up at the sleeves.

Then the only sounds in the darkness were a heavy

thump in the bedroom and the squeak of the rusty wheel-barrow axle. Some time later, from the area of the barn, came the uneven gnashing of the chicken feed grinder working on something hard, amid the loud, thoroughly satisfied grunting and rooting of the pigs.

An hour later Cyrila was standing on the farmhouse porch. She had on her flower-print dress again, and behind her every light in the house blazed. A far-off wail, like a forlorn siren, rolled through the night. She stood listening to the approaching thunder of the distant train, heard it slow momentarily, then with a blast of new thunder begin to regain its speed. Gradually it left her in silence. She unconsciously smoothed the dress over her hips, sighed, then turned and walked into the house. The midnight train roared westward through the inky darkness—but Ulman wasn't on it.

AMEN!

by Ed Lacy

I'm a true believer, you understand, in my own way but not much of a church-going man. No, I'm not going to argue religion with you, or with my wife, either. You see, one night the wife comes home with this eight-inch statue of Saint Christopher, made of heavy plastic and with a magnetic base. "It's for your truck, Joe," she said. "He's the patron saint of drivers and travelers and I'd feel better if you keep this on your dashboard."

So there it is; I been driving since I was twelve, I'm a darn good driver, and I don't need any statues to help me at the wheel. Also, I know better than to argue with the wife about a thing like *this*. I merely thanked her, didn't even mention that my boss would certainly tell me to keep it off the dashboard, it's against insurance regulations.

Sure enough, the following morning, as I'm taking my truck out of the warehouse, the boss said, "Okay, Joe, you want a St. Christopher, wear one of them medals around your fat neck. But take that off the truck. I don't want no accidents."

"He's supposed to prevent accidents," I said brightly and sarcastically.

"I'm talking about an accident to *you,* stupid. You run into a heavy bump, or somebody rams into you and WHAM! that little statue is going to fly off the dashboard with bullet speed, maybe knock your eyes out. And if the insurance company learns about it, good-bye any possible compensation for you. And you drive like a hotrod kid anyway, so move it!"

Frankly I didn't give a hoot about the statue anyway, so I worked things out like this: entering and leaving the garage I kept the statue in the glove compartment, so the boss won't bug me. Once I was rolling, I stuck the St. Christopher back on the dashboard only because in driving around town I sometimes pass the wife out shopping, and if she saw I didn't have the statue she'd bug me worse than my boss. And she's the gal who can do it, too.

Things went like that for a couple of months and this morning, when the boss handed me my trip ticket, he said, "Be careful, Joe, you're carrying a bonded load, $82,000 worth of transistor radios. Try to remember you're at the wheel of a truck, not a jet plane."

I told him a few things—when I was a block away from the warehouse, sticking the statue on the dash-board. The traffic thinned as I reached the edge of town. I was headed for a company sort of in the coun-try, which would make for a nice day's driving and no chance of being stuck with a second trip. Stopping for a traffic light a snappy sports roadster with two young guys in it drove up on my right. The taller guy called out, "How far to Newton, pal?"

"Newton?" I laughed. "You're driving in the wrong direction. Look, at the next intersection, make a left and follow that to the next . . ."

"Wait up, I can't hear you," the tall guy said, getting out of the car and coming up to the window of my truck cab.

He should have heard me; we were the only cars waiting for the light. "I said, at the next intersection you make a . . ." My voice died as I found myself look-ing into a very ugly .38 pistol.

Sliding into the seat beside me the tall guy said, "Do as you're told, truck jockey, and you don't get hurt. Try anything, and you're a dead hero! Drive, I'll tell you where to go."

I fully knew my chances of ever being a day older were slim. A hijacker drives the truck to some isolated spot where he has another truck waiting. After unload-ing and loading the stuff, the next step is always to slug the driver and/or drop his body off on some lonely road.

The light turned green and the gunman told me to drive on. At the next crossing, he had me make a right turn. In the mirror I saw his partner following us in the sports car. I was trying to think and getting only zeros, when ahead of us I saw another crossing, but with a traf-fic cop and lights. For a second my hopes went into orbit, until the goon jammed his gun into my side and snarled, "So there's a cop, so you play it cool! One wrong movement and you get the lead treatment! I ain't kidding."

I didn't doubt it, either; he was a hell of a snarler. I just nodded, sweat running down my big face. If I went through the light, ran the truck up on the side-walk, did *anything* to make the policeman mad I might wrestle the punk, try to hold him until the officer came up. But the barrel of his gun, which seemed to be bor-ing a hole in my kidney, told me I wouldn't have a chance. And the other hood, in the sports car, would take out the cop, gun him down.

The light turned green as we approached and I drove on, wanting to scream for help, but my throat was dry as sand. Suddenly a kid came busting out of a weedy lot and raced across the street. Jamming the brakes on with reflex action, my truck lurched to a sudden stop, skidding sideways across the road. I didn't touch the kid but I saw St. Christopher carom off the windshield on the impact of the sudden stop, strike the gunman's eye, blinding him for a second. I dug my elbow into his side and grabbed his gun as he crumpled forward in the seat, mouth sucking air.

Jumping out of the truck, I saw the other punk trying to turn his snappy car around, since my truck was blocking the road. The cop was running towards us. I tried to yell it was a hold-up—but not a sound came forth. But the cop already had his gun out, probably because I was still holding the tall punk's gun in my own trembling hand.

Well, the two punks were sent up, the cop was promoted, and for saving them $82,000 the insurance company wrote me a ginger-peachy letter of commendation.

Of course I still don't go for that statue bit. But looking at the slightly crumpled St. Christopher statue on my dashboard, I don't know; I just may even go to church ... one of these days.

CONFLICT OF INTEREST

by James Holding

I had no trouble keeping Matheny in sight, even among
the sidewalk crowds along Queen's Boulevard. He
stood five inches over six feet and he threw his left foot
like a horse with bone spavin in a hock joint. I was
half a block behind him, though, and when he came
to 108th Street and turned off the Boulevard, I had to
hurry. I got to the corner in time to see him duck into
a bar-and-grill down toward the Inn.

I followed him inside after a peek through the front
window of the place showed me that he was sitting by
himself at a side table for four with his back to the door.
I could see his hatless streaked-blond head sticking up
over the booth partition.

I climbed up on a stool at the bar where I could see
him in the bar mirror but he couldn't see me. I thought
he was waiting for somebody to join him and I wanted
to know who. I ordered a plain tonic water from the
bartender and nursed it. I like tonic water better with
gin in it, who doesn't, but it gives me indigestion. Anyway, when you're trying to cut in on people like Matheny, you've got to go easy on the sauce.

After fifteen minutes, I figured I was wrong about
him meeting somebody. Nobody showed up at his table,
and when a waitress went to him to see if he wanted

another beer, he told her, "Yeah, with my dinner. I want a sirloin steak, rare, and french fries and catsup on the side. No salad."

That was enough for me. I beckoned to the bartender, paid for the tonic water and left. If he was going to eat dinner and have another beer, I ought to have a good half hour to myself. I went back to Queen's Boulevard. Up by the florist's shop near the 8th Avenue subway stairs, a guy was passing out leaflets of some kind to the pedestrians. Not many were taking them. I turned west and walked fast.

Matheny lived in a rented room over a bakery shop. I went up the narrow staircase from the street. One look at the lock on the door at the top of the steps made me feel a lot better right away. A baby could have picked it with his rattle handle. I used a plastic calendar card and some pressure. When the door swung open under this simple routine, I began to feel bad again, because nobody with any sense, much less a hard case like Matheny, would leave very much loot in a pad as easy to bust into as that—and loot was what I was after. I knew he had it, but I didn't know where he kept it. That was my trouble.

As long as I was there, though, I gave the place my best treatment. It didn't take me very long.

There was nothing in Matheny's one-room mansion except a broken-down studio couch pulled out into a bed and left that way, with dirty sheets partly hidden by the couch cover; a scarred chest of drawers with the drawers not closed tight; an easy chair whose fake leather upholstery was burned in one place and stained in another; a reading lamp on a rickety table beside the chair, with sections of the daily newspaper scattered around it on the carpet; and the carpet itself which missed being wall-to-wall by three feet on every side and missed being new by about thirty years. A telephone was on the floor in a corner.

There wasn't any likely place in the room where Matheny could have hidden the money. It would be kind of bulky, being in cash, and would take up a good bit of room. I went over the furniture, walls, ceiling, the floor under the carpet, even the base of the telephone. I didn't find a thing.

The telephone made me feel better again, though, because it looked pretty clean compared to everything else in the room, and maybe that meant Matheny had put it in after he rented the room. If he had, that meant he was expecting somebody to call him or he was to call somebody, and that somebody could be whoever was holding the cash for him, or was going to tip him when the heat was off, or meet him for a split-up some-where, or something connected with the cash. Matheny had stashed the loot somewhere, and I wanted it.

After I finished with the room, I gave his bathroom a going-over, too, but no luck there, either. Matheny wasn't the kind of dope to hide his loot in the water tank.

I looked at my watch and saw I'd been away from the bar-and-grill where Matheny was having his sirloin rare for twenty minutes. I was still on the safe side of any chance he might come home and catch me. All the same, I thought I'd better get out. I straightened every-thing up, then went over to the telephone in the corner to see if I'd remembered the number right. I figured maybe I could use it later on, someway.

Just as I bent over the telephone, it rang.

I stared at the phone for a second and it rang again. A lot of things went through my head in a hurry. The one that came out winner was that maybe this call had something to do with the money. So I picked up the receiver, held the mouthpiece away from my face and said, "Hello." Nobody said anything for a count of three, and I couldn't hear anybody breathing at the other end. Wrong number, I thought.

Then a man's voice, indistinct against a faint roar of background noise, said, "Boulevard 3-2459?"

That was Matheny's number. I held the receiver away from my mouth again and said, "Yeah." I waited. A little more of nothing happened next.

Finally, the voice said, "Three-oh-six, four-two." I heard a click at the other end of the wire.

Great. I hung up. I said *that* number to myself a couple of times, fixing it in my mind. Don't ask me why. I told myself I was a jerk for not asking the guy who was calling. I'd never latch onto Matheny's dough that way. Come to that, maybe the guy on the phone was a jerk, too. He hadn't even asked me if I was Matheny.

I wiped off the telephone receiver, just to be safe, and got out of there.

Back on 108th, the guy passing out leaflets was working the other side of the street. He stepped in front of me and said, "Take a leaflet, sir, for the good of your soul." I took it and shoved it into my pocket and kept on walking. It was something about a religious sect called Theosophists United, whoever they were.

I crossed over to the other sidewalk and looked through the window of the bar-and-grill where I'd left Matheny. He was still there. I went on by, walked through the Long Island Railroad underpass and went into the Inn.

I needed a drink and dinner myself. The Inn isn't cheap, but I've always liked to live it up when I've got

the price. Sitting at the bar, though, I got to thinking
about my indigestion again, and ended up ordering
another plain tonic water with a squeeze of lime instead
of gin. I washed down a peptic tablet with the first swal-
low, and worked my shoulders to make my gun ride
a little easier under my coat.

While I downed the tonic and had dinner, I thought
about the number I'd heard over Matheny's telephone:
30642. It might have meant something to Matheny, but
it sure didn't meant anything to me. I went through some
possibilities. It wasn't a telephone number, not enough
digits. Too high a number for a check locker in an airport or railroad station. And certainly too high for a
safe-deposit box in a bank.

You can see how my mind was running. I wanted
the number to have something to do with Matheny's
loot; a clue to where he'd stashed it, or who was holding it, or where he was going to meet the others who
had been in on the job with him.

I came up with nothing except a full feeling from the
veal parmigiana I had for dinner, so I paid my check
and went out into the lobby of the Inn.

A couple of stewardesses and pilots from La Guardia
Airport were signing in at the desk. They were still in
uniform, kidding around, not a care in the world. I
gave the two good-looking birds the eye and that did
it.

I could be going at my number all wrong. I was saying to myself three-oh, and then a pause, and then the
last three numbers, six-four-two. Then I recalled the
guy on the phone had said the first three numbers together, then a pause, then the last two numbers.

Seeing the airline people triggered it. The number
could be an airplane flight number, followed by a

seat number. Flight 306, seat 42, and the background noise behind the guy's voice on Matheny's phone could have been the roar of an airport terminal.

I shut myself into a telephone booth, looked up Flight Information at Kennedy and dialed it.

A girl's voice answered. "Flight Information."

I said, "Have you got a flight number 306 listed on your schedule anywhere?"

"What airline?" she asked.

"I don't know. That's why I'm calling."

"Do you know when it's scheduled, sir?"

"I don't know that, either."

She laughed. "Do you happen to know where it's going?"

"No."

"Or where it's coming from?"

"Just the flight number," I said.

"Well, if you'll hold on a minute, I'll try to find it for you." She put a lot of patience into her voice.

I held on. She was gone less than a minute. "Here we are," she told me. "TGA Jetstar Flight 306, Pittsburgh, Indianapolis, Kansas City, out of Kennedy at 10:30 tomorrow morning. That sound like it?"

"Thanks a million," I said.

I looked up TGA Reservations in the book and put another dime in the slot. My hand shook a bit.

"Your flight 306 tomorrow morning," I said to the girl who answered. "Any seats left?"

"Yes, sir. To Kansas City?"

I took a chance. "To Pittsburgh," I said. Pittsburgh was where Matheny had knocked over the bank.

"First class or coach?"

"Coach." I like to live it up, but not that much. Besides, seat 42 ought to be in the coach section.

"Right, sir," the girl said. "Your name, please?"

"Arthur Matheny." I spelled it for her.

"Your ticket will be waiting for you at the TGA counter, Mr. Matheny. And thank you for calling TGA."

"Not at all," I said, and hung up. My heartburn kicked up suddenly, like hot steam in my throat. I got out a tablet and chewed it before I left the telephone booth. Heartburn or no heartburn, I was feeling fine. Things were beginning to move. I was pretty sure I was on my way to Matheny's dough—or some of it, anyway.

Seat 42 was a window seat on the left side about half-way up. I had a seat two rows behind it and on the aisle.

The stewardess who checked me in was a dish. Her hair under the uniform cap was dark brown and so were her eyes. Suntanned, she had a nice nose and a figure that didn't go straight up and down any place, as far as I could see, and I was looking. She gave me a perfunctory smile when she checked me off on her clipboard.

The plane wasn't a quarter full when we took off, and that was all right with me.

Seat 42 was empty. I figured it might be, with such a small load. Would Matheny have asked for that particular seat? I didn't think so. It would have drawn attention to the seat. He wouldn't want that. He'd probably have played it by ear once he was on the plane, the way I meant to.

We weren't airborne more than half an hour before the stewardesses started passing out snacks and offering drinks. I didn't take any because of my heartburn, but I said a few words to the stewardess with the Raquel Welch shape when she bent over me with her tray.

"How long to Pittsburgh?" I asked her. She smelled like carnations.

She laughed. "You're almost there. It's less than half an hour more. You sure you won't have anything?"

I told her no, I'd just finished breakfast. She seemed in no hurry to move on, so I said, "Not many passengers today."

"It's always light on Mondays." She leaned a little closer to me. Carnations again. "To tell you the truth, I'm just as glad. Gives us a chance to rest up a little bit after the weekend." She flashed the smile at me, not so perfunctory this time.

"I haven't flown this route before," I said. "Is it all right if I move over to a window seat and take a look out?"

"Of course," she said. "Take any vacant seat you want."

"Thanks." I stood up, took my flight bag from the overhead rack, squeezed past the stewardess in the aisle, which was pleasant, went forward two rows and slid by a gray-haired man's knees into seat 42. The gray-haired man was asleep.

Holding my flight bag in my lap, I leaned over and looked out the window beside me at what we were passing below. I guess it was the Allegheny Mountains. It looked like a green skin dented with wrinkles.

I wasn't really interested in the view, anyway. After three minutes of staring at it, I had a crick in my neck and I turned away from the window. The stewardess was up ahead, not noticing me. The gray-haired guy next door was still asleep. I fumbled a copy of the airline's in-flight magazine, *Jetstar,* from the pocket on the seat ahead of me, opened it and pretended to read. I hoped I looked convincing.

With the magazine and my flight bag hiding my

movements in case my neighbor woke up, I used my left hand, the one next to the window, to explore seat 42.

I didn't know what I was looking for. Some kind of a hiding place, probably, but a simple one, where Matheny could find whatever it was he was going to pick up without too much trouble . . . a message or a map or cash. It could be anything, but I was betting on cash. Cash was what turned Matheny on.

If I hadn't known there was something to look for in seat 42, I'd never have found it. Only the overlap, where the long thin patch of seat material had been applied over the upholstery, gave it away. My fingers, sliding along the curve of the seat where it went under my knees, found a slight unevenness in the smooth, tight-stretched nylon seat covering, and I knew right away I had it.

I picked at one of the ends of the patch with a fingernail. It came loose for about half an inch, peeling back like an adhesive bandage off a cut finger.

I checked the man next to me. His eyes were still closed, so I risked a quick look down past my magazine and flight bag at the little flap of material I'd pulled loose. The light wasn't too good, but it looked like an exact match for the seat-covering material; same color, same texture, same amount of fade. It was a neat job down under the front curve of the foam rubber seat where nobody would notice it in a million years. I pulled at the flap of material and it peeled back another inch. The adhesive it was stuck on with was the kind that stays sticky. The flap I'd raised stuck to my fingers like chewing gum.

I peeled back another inch, still pretending to read my *Jetstar* magazine. When I could work my forefinger and thumb loose from the stickum on the patch, I shoved them through the slit in the upholstery under the patch, and felt a cut-out hollow in the three inch seat pad inside. In the hollow, my fingers came up against the straight edge of a small flat package. Bingo!

I took my fingers away from the hole in the seat and brought them up in my lap where I told them to turn a page in *Jetstar* while I ran a check of the plane passengers and crew. Nobody seemed to be caring whether I lived or died or stole Matheny's money. At least nobody was looking my way. The old gent next to me was sleeping so hard now, he'd slipped sideways away from me and was practically falling into the aisle.

I dropped my left hand out of sight again, grabbed the front edge of the flat package in two fingers and worked it out of the seat. I brought it up slow and easy into my lap under my flight bag and slid it into one of the bag's outside pockets, covering the move with the magazine in my other hand. Then I stuck the patch back down over the slit in the upholstery.

Just in time, too. The flight deck gave us the word we were letting down for Pittsburgh and the passengers all went through the belt-fastening bit except for the sleeper beside me. The carnation-smelling stewardess straightened him up and fastened his belt for him, waking him up in the process. When I fastened mine, I transferred the flat package from the pocket of my flight bag to the inside of it, under my clean shirt and electric shaver.

I was excited. I figured the flat package had about the right dimensions to hold a couple of stacks of bills maybe three quarters of an inch high. And that could come to a bundle of dough if the bills were all hundreds, say. Twenty or twenty-five grand.

We floated across some power lines and a super-highway and made a smooth landing at Pittsburgh. I unfastened my seat belt, grabbed my flight bag in one hot hand, stumbled over my neighbor's knees again, and was all ready to leave the minute the door was opened. Only six other passengers were getting off in Pittsburgh, I noticed, unless some millionaires were descending from first class. I said good-bye and thanks to the pretty stewardess and ducked down the steps. There was a handful of people at the exit gate waiting for friends or relatives from the plane, but I didn't give them a second look.

I should have.

I had no luggage except my flight bag. I saw the word "Men" on a door in the waiting room inside the gate. I headed for it without looking back. The package was burning a hole in my flight bag.

In the men's room I stepped into a compartment, locked the door, brought out the package. It was done up in brown wrapping paper. I gently loosened one end of the paper, expecting to see edges of currency stacked solid. I didn't. What I saw was the end of a shallow blue box. I slid the box out of the wrapping, fiddled with the catch and lifted the lid. All that got me was a look at a piece of chamois skin—the kind you wash windows with, but softer. Impatiently I flipped back the flap of chamois and finally saw what I had.

Not cash. Diamonds.

The blue box was full of them. Square cuts, marquises, pear shapes and rounds, packed between layers of chamois skin and throwing sparks like a rhinestone G-string under a baby spot.

Nice surprise from Matheny. I don't know much about diamonds, but that tray of ice could be worth ten times as much as the two little stacks of currency I'd been hoping for. There wasn't a stone in the collection smaller than two carats, and some were jumbos.

I closed the box, slid it back into the wrapping paper, folded the loose flap in. Then I shoved the box into my flight bag and left the men's room.

The escalator that led from the field waiting room up to the main floor of the terminal was just outside the men's room. I stepped on it and started up to get a ticket on the next plane to New York. A voice behind me said, "Matheny."

I turned my head. A short, fat, broken-nosed type was riding the escalator step below mine. He wasn't giving me the big smile of an old friend, but he wasn't looking hostile, either. He was occupying the whole width of the escalator belt, with a hand on both rails. I couldn't reverse my field, that was for sure.

I said, "Oh, there you are. I wondered when somebody would show up. I was waiting around for you."

Another voice, light and feathery, pulled my head around the other way. "In the men's?" it said.

This one was slight and blond and dressed in a sky-blue sport jacket over red-checked slacks. Unlike his clothes, his eyes didn't have any color in them and they didn't focus quite straight.

I said to him, "I didn't think you'd leave."

The fat one moved up beside me. His buddy stood facing us, riding up the escalator backwards. He said, "You're not Matheny."

"Am I supposed to be?"

"Your stewardess said so." The fat one crowded me against the escalator rail. "We checked with her when Matheny didn't show. The first man off the plane, she said. That's you. And you ain't Matheny."

"I knew that all along," I said, grinning at him. "Matheny couldn't come."

"Why not?"

"Sick."

"What do you mean, sick? Matheny don't get sick. He's healthy as a horse."

"Not now he isn't." I said. "He went to the hospital yesterday."

Two pairs of eyes stared at me as though they thought it might be my fault. The pretty boy stumbled when the escalator reached the top level and bumped him backwards off his step. He almost fell, but I reached out and caught him as Fatso and I stepped off. He didn't thank me, but closed in on my right side and we walked three abreast down the long corridor of the air terminal.

The gaily dressed one made sketchy introductions. "I'm Brad," he said, "and that's Leo." We walked a few more steps. "So who are you?"

"Matheny, for this job," I said.

Brad said, "You got the package?"

"What do you think?"

"I think you damn well better have it, or it'll be too bad for you. And Matheny." This was Leo.

"Then let's say I've got it, okay?" I flipped my flight bag. "Where are we going?"

The slender one hitched a shoulder. "To Mitch," he said. "Where else?"

"Matheny didn't tell me about Mitch."

"What did he tell you?"

"Told me somebody would pay me five G's for making a pickup and delivery in his place. That somebody would meet me at the Pittsburgh airport. And if it didn't work out, I could keep the package."

Leo laughed. "That Matheny," he chortled, "he's a million laughs." He sobered suddenly and said, "You a friend of Matheny's?"

"You might say so, yes."

"Where'd you know him?" The colorless eyes on my

right gave me a crooked scrutiny.

"I'll tell Mitch," I said.

We came out of the main entrance to the airport terminal building and headed for a big parking lot off to the right.

"I'll carry your bag," Brad offered.

I shook my head. "I'll carry it. As far as Mitch, anyway. It isn't heavy."

"Mercy," said Brad in his high tenor, "he's touchy, isn't he?"

"Nervous is what he is," Leo laughed. "Over this way."

They shepherded me into the parking lot and down a long row of cars to a black sedan at the end. Leo got under the wheel. Brad, behind me, said, "Sit in the middle." I climbed in and sat above the hump in the floor with my flight bag in my lap. The front seat wasn't meant for three. I didn't complain. Brad climbed in after me and slammed his door.

Leo tooled the car out of the parking lot and turned into a four-lane highway heading east. Once we got rolling, Brad said in his feathery voice, "I'll carry your bag now."

I looked down, and he had a gun in his lap, aimed in the general direction of my appendix. I looked up again, into his colorless eyes. "If you insist," I said.

Brad took my flight bag and tossed it into the back seat. He just wanted to make a point.

Leo said, "That's sensible. Brad gets kind of touchy himself sometimes."

Brad's lips lifted and he exposed very white teeth that could have been false in a sweet smile. "Good gracious," he said, "do you know something, Leo? I believe this friend of Matheny's is armed. Mitch wouldn't like that."

"Left armpit," Leo said. "I felt it on the escalator."

Brad reached over and relieved me of my gun. Then he put his own away, looking straight into my eyes the whole time. I was glad to have his gun out of sight, to tell the truth. Brad dressed and talked like a flit, but his funny eyes told me he liked to use that gun.

We took a left off the highway after a while and followed that road for a few miles at an easy sixty till we came to a river. As we went over it on a high suspension bridge, I said, "Is this the beautiful Ohio?" and got nothing but a grunt from Leo in reply.

Pretty soon we went east again on a road bordering the river, rolled through a little hick-town business section and turned north up a winding road that climbed the steep bluff behind the town. I saw a roadside sign that said "Coraopolis Heights." As Leo worked up higher and higher on the bluff, I could look down and see the river shining below us.

Brad wanted to make another point. "You still didn't tell us your name," he said in his delicate well-bred way.

"Let it wait," Leo told him.

We turned into a concrete driveway toward the top of the hill. Leo touched a gadget on his sun visor and the wide door of a two-car garage rolled up and let him snuggle the sedan in beside a red convertible.

I got only a quick look at the house as we drove in. It was built into the cliff above the garage, and two or three stories high, I couldn't tell which, not counting the garage level. There was no lawn and no fence. The ground was too steep for anything but trees to hang onto. There were plenty of those, though, all around the house, growing close in.

I said, "Is this where Mitch lives?" and crawled out of the car after Brad.

"Yeah," Leo answered. "Some cottage, huh?"

Brad opened the back door of the sedan and took out my flight bag, giving me a creepy look as he did it. We went up a couple of steps from the garage to a square hall by the front door of the house, and stepped into an elevator that took us up one flight into a big livingroom.

The livingroom was nicely furnished, with a bar finished in leather and nail heads at one end, an open fireplace at the other. One whole wall was made of sliding glass panels. Outside the glass wall was a terrace with wrought iron furniture scattered around and a fine view of the river. The terrace was really the roof of the garage.

A big guy wearing hornrims and a neat goatee was sitting in one of the terrace chairs by a round umbrella table, watching us as we came through the livingroom and out onto the terrace. Mitch, no doubt. His ears were small and set low on his head and tight against it. He had reddish-brown hair, and bare feet stuck into sandals. He was wearing jeans and an open-necked shirt and he had a French paperback open on his lap. If I had to make a guess, I'd have said he was a professor cutting his own classes.

Leo started to say something, but Mitch interrupted him. "Who's this?" He looked at me when he said it.

"Matheny's sick," Brad explained. "This guy came instead. At least, that's the way he tells it." He gestured with my flight bag which he held in his left hand, leaving his right hand free to draw his gun, maybe.

Mitch took the flight bag, zipped it open, rummaged around in it and brought up the package wrapped in brown paper. His scholarly pan got a relieved look on it.

Leo said softly, "If that ain't it, Mitch, he hid it in the men's room at the airport. That's where we picked him up. Every place else, since he left the plane, we been on him good."

Mitch didn't answer right away. He was busy tearing the wrapping off the box. When he got the lid up and turned back the chamois skin, he looked at the diamonds for a minute. Brad and Leo gawked at them, too. I did myself. Under the open sunlight, they looked even better than they did under the men's room fluorescents.

Mitch got some heart into his voice. "This is it, Leo," he said. "This is definitely it." Leo sat down. Mitch closed the box and looked at me directly for the first time, as though I could be a person after all. "I owe you for this," he said with disarming candor. "Mr. . . .?" He paused for an answer.

"Smith," I said. "I was glad to do Matheny the favor. He told me I'd have five G's coming."

Mitch frowned but nodded. "Fair enough, Mr. Smith. You'll get it."

I needled him a little. "From the looks of that box, you could afford to pay me more than five."

Mitch didn't react one way or the other. He said, "What happened to Matheny?"

"Busted appendix, I think. We were playing gin yesterday afternoon when it hit him. He doubled up like a hunch bettor—"

Mitch cut in. "Where?"

"Where?"

"Yes. Where were you playing gin?"

"At his place," I said easily, "in Forest Hills."

He frowned again. "Go on."

"His pains got worse. The phone rang once and he could hardly answer it. But he did, and after that, he asked me to stick around for a while just in case. So I did. By seven o'clock he was hurting bad enough to know it was something serious. I told him what it was.

Just like me when my appendix busted once. You get a high fever and pains you wouldn't believe. I told him he ought to get to a doctor or the hospital before something let go on him. He says okay, if I'll do him a favor and make this pickup and delivery. Told me the setup and said I'd get five grand. Then I called him a cab and sent him off to the hospital."

"What hospital?"

"Search me. I told the cabbie to take him to the nearest one." That seemed safe enough. I was pretty sure Matheny wouldn't have registered under his own name anyway, even if he *had* gone to a hospital.

"Why didn't you go with him?"

"He wanted me to get started on a reservation for the plane this morning. He said he'd be okay." I shrugged my shoulders. It felt funny with my gun's weight gone. "Maybe he's okay and maybe he isn't. All I know is, it's six-two-and-even he had a busted appendix. And he promised me five grand. Let's not forget that."

Mitch nodded to a chair. "Sit down, Mr. Smith. Brad, get Mr. Smith a drink, will you? What'll you have, Mr. Smith?"

"Plain tonic water if you've got it," I said. "Alcohol gives me heartburn."

Brad went off toward the livingroom bar. Mitch swiveled his eyes at Leo without saying anything. Leo got up and went into the house.

I called after him, "Boulevard 3-2459, area code 412. But he won't be there, Leo. I guarantee it."

Mitch laughed. "We'll check anyway. Okay? You been a friend of Matheny's very long, Smith?" No 'Mister' now, I noticed. It should have sounded patronizing from this egghead type, but it didn't. Just friendly. Mitch had a way with him. I figured maybe he was be-

ginning to believe me. With the diamonds in his lap
and my knowing Matheny's hideout and telephone number, there was no reason why he shouldn't. I hoped.

Brad came back with a glass of tonic water in his
hand and a sneer on his face. Probably thought *I* was
a queer if I drank that slop. He didn't sit down after he
handed me my drink, but went and stood by the terrace
rail, a little behind me on my left, where a clump of
young ash trees hugged the terrace. I figured from that
that they still didn't exactly trust me.

I figured right. Mitch repeated his question about
how long I'd known Matheny. I said, "Quite a while."

"Since when?"

I took a chance. "Since Raiford."

"You were in prison with him?" Mitch was surprised.

"Yeah. The stretch he did for armed robbery in
Jacksonville." That was safe, too.

Mitch fiddled with the box of diamonds. "Funny
Matheny never mentioned you to me."

"Or me," Brad fluted behind me.

"Nothing funny about it," I said. "I never worked
with him on a job. Never even saw him after Raiford
until I was casing a thing in Forest Hills yesterday and
ran into him on the street." I grinned. "You can't miss
Art Matheny. The way he sticks above everybody else
and throws his left foot when he walks. I was glad to
see him."

"Why?" Mitch didn't take his eyes off me. "After all
those years?"

I tried to look embarrassed. "I figured maybe I could
touch him for a century. My luck has been lousy late-
ly. And Matheny looked prosperous."

Leo came back to the terrace. He looked at Mitch
and shook his head. I hadn't expected that Matheny

would answer the phone. The chances were against it. But I felt relieved, all the same.

Mitch said to Leo, "Matheny ever mention a friend named Smith to you?"

"What's your first name?" Leo asked me. "Smith ain't enough. Everybody has a friend named Smith, don't they?" A clown.

"Firedoor," I said. "Firedoor Smith."

Leo laughed. "Matheny never mentioned no Firedoor Smith to me," he told Mitch. Then he asked me, "How come Firedoor?"

I said, "I work apartments and hotels. So I use firedoors to make my scores, that's all there is to it."

Even Mitch smiled at that. "Then a pickup in an airplane is right down your alley."

"Right," I said.

Mitch put a finger under his red beard and scratched his neck. I thought I knew what was bothering him. Matheny had probably been under orders to stay strictly doggo in New York until he got that telephone call I'd taken for him. No social contacts like gin rummy with an old lag allowed. So how come I'd been with Matheny when he took sick?

Mitch's next words hinted I was right. "Lucky for us you happened to be there when Matheny got the cramps."

"Well, I ran into him by a bakery, just as he was going up some stairs alongside. It turned out he lived there." I made a face. "What a dump. But I figured it was just temporary. While the heat died down from his last job, probably."

"What *was* his last job?"

"He didn't say, and I didn't ask him. If you know Matheny, you ought to know he's a tight-mouth." Mitch said nothing, so I went on. "Speaking of luck, it was lucky for *me* I happened to be Johnny-on-the-spot when Matheny's appendix busted. Five G's are more sugar than I've seen all at once for more than three years, would you believe that? I *need* it, man! That's why I kind of forced myself to be invited into Matheny's pad and tried to swing a loan over the gin rummy game. And I guess that's why Matheny knew I wouldn't cross him on this pickup thing. Not with five G's in sight when I was flat."

"He give you the dough for your airplane ticket?" Brad said.

"I used the dough I won from him at gin. He's a lousy player."

Mitch said to Brad, "Knock it off, Brad." And to me, "What did you think you had in this box?" He tapped the diamonds.

I looked him straight in the eye. "Horse."

He blinked. "You didn't open the box while you were in the men's room, did you?"

I said no.

Mitch said, "One end of the wrapping was loose."

"It tore when I pulled it out of the airplane seat."

He leaned back in his chair. "Don't hand me that, Firedoor. There isn't a man alive who could resist looking into a package he'd been paid five grand to collect —if he had the chance. And you had the chance. You took a peek, didn't you?"

"Well . . ."

"And when you saw it was diamonds, you thought you'd go into business for yourself, didn't you?"

I looked guilty, I guess, because he laughed out loud.

"I know how these things go, Firedoor, believe me. I'm not a psychology professor for nothing."

I said, "What!"

"Currently between jobs," he said, and laughed again. "Ask Brad and Leo why they work for me. It's because I know how people's minds work, and make money from it. And because I know how people's minds work, all my people are not only safer but more successful working for me than for themselves."

This guy had to be a little nuts, I thought. I looked at Leo and his battered mug was solemnly nodding agreement to Mitch's brag. I said, *"All* your people? You got more than Matheny and these two here?" I put respect into the question.

"Who do you think bought these diamonds for me from a jewel thief in Amsterdam?" Mitch said quietly. "And who do you think secreted them in the airplane seat for Matheny to pick up? And who do you think tipped off Matheny what flight to catch today, and what seat the stones were in?"

Amsterdam, that explained some of it. One of Mitch's people in Europe bought a ticket for New York on a TGA plane, hid the diamonds in his seat cushion during the flight over and covered up the slit in the upholstery with a pre-prepared patch. When he arrived at Kennedy in New York, he left the diamonds on the plane and went through customs inspection like any other innocent tourist. Then Matheny was tipped off to the flight and seat number and was to go aboard that plane's first domestic flight, collect the diamonds and take them off the plane at Pittsburgh, because there's no U.S. Customs inspection in Pittsburgh for passengers on domestic flights. A very cozy setup.

In answer to Mitch's questions, I asked, "Who?" He seemed to expect it.

"My people," he said. "And that's merely a sampling. I have excellent connections all over Europe and America, and excellent people to help me exploit them. We all make a very nice living, don't we, boys?" he appealed to Brad and Leo.

I was impressed. I said wistfully, "I could use my five G's, in that case. A boss smuggler like you wouldn't even miss it."

Mitch laughed. "Smuggling's only part of it. I'm running sort of a conglomerate here, you might say. And all my subsidiaries are showing a nice profit at the moment."

"Mitch!" Brad protested in his high voice.

Mitch waved a hand at him. "Don't worry so much, Brad. I know what I'm doing." He turned back to me. "A little smuggling, a little bank robbery, a little car theft for those poor deprived people in South America . . . We try our hands at anything that pays well, Firedoor."

"Wow!" I said in simple admiration.

Mitch patted the diamonds. "I like the way you handled this pickup for Matheny on very short notice. It took brains and a lot of cool to bring it off so smoothly your first time out of the gate. I can use brains and cool like that. Would you consider working for me?"

Brad started to say something. Mitch gave him a sharp look and he shut up. Leo's broken-nosed face was as deadpan as ever. I said, "Hell, Mr. Mitchell, you've got to be kidding!" I made it plain I hoped he wasn't.

Brad muttered something under his breath.

"I'm not kidding. I might activate another subsidiary with you as chief executive officer, Firedoor." He laughed. "Our hotel and apartment division. I have some ideas along those lines that could be turned into important money if applied to just the right objectives."

The telephone rang in the livingroom and Leo went to answer it.

I said, "This doesn't affect the five G's I've already got coming?"

"Of course not."

"Then I'll take the job, Mr. Mitchell. And glad to get it."

Leo walked out on the terrace.

"Who was it?" Mitch asked him.

"Ruby."

"Yes?"

Leo broke his deadpan rule. He threw me a real disgusted look. "She says no hospital in Queens admitted an acute appendicitis patient last night after seven o'clock. Or even treated one with a bad gut pain. Or even any patient six foot, five inches tall. And there ain't no Matheny registered in any of them, either. Even the private ones."

All of a sudden I felt chilly. Leo wasn't as dumb as he looked.

Mitch clicked his tongue politely. Brad stirred at my back. I thought I heard the safety on his gun click off, but it could have been my imagination. I didn't turn to look.

Mitch said sadly, "Why, Mr. Smith, I'm afraid you haven't been leveling with us. At least it looks that way. But we can't be sure, can we, until we hear from Matheny?"

"*If* we ever hear from Matheny," Brad said. "We're sure enough to suit me right now, Mitch. Give me this monkey. I'll take care of him."

"Presently, Brad." Mitch spoke to him like a mother soothing a bad-tempered baby. "We can't be precipitate.

That's one of my cardinal rules. You know that. Meanwhile, I suggest we put him in our little hideaway on the top floor. Use the elevator." He laughed with enjoyment. "And lock the firedoor."

Brad said, "That's a waste of time, Mitch. Let me have him now."

"Shut up," Leo said, and to me, "Let's go, stupid." He came over and grabbed one of my arms in a big paw, making me spill some of my tonic water. Brad closed in on my other arm, very military. Now I could see that he *did* have his gun out and the safety *was* off.

They were helping me out of my chair when the phone rang again. Only it wasn't the phone. It was a signal from an intercom. Leo, at a nod from Mitch, let go of my arm, went to a grid beside the elevator in the livingroom, and spoke into it.

"What is it?" Mitch called to him.

"Somebody at the front door asking for Matheny," Leo reported.

"For Matheny?" Mitch was startled. "Cops?"

"John says no," Leo answered. John must be another of Mitch's 'people' I hadn't seen. "It's a chick," Leo said. "By herself."

"Well, well," Mitch murmured to me softly. "So there's a girl in on this with you?" He called to Leo, "Tell John to send her up."

I put down my tonic glass. I didn't want the rest of the stuff anyway. I planted my feet to make a good try for Brad's gun, but something round and cold came against the back of my neck, so I thought the hell with it, and relaxed again—as much as my heartburn would let me.

I went back to feeling lousy again when I saw the chick who came tail-switching out onto the terrace with Leo, pushing a faint smell of carnations ahead of her: the stacked stewardess from flight 306. She'd ditched her TGA cap and wings somewhere, but she still wore her uniform blouse and skirt, and she was still a dish.

I hoped she wasn't mixed up with this crummy crew, a nice girl like her. But if she wasn't, she stood a fine chance of getting hit in the head along with me. I said, "I thought you'd be in Kansas City by now, baby."

She nodded to me without smiling. "Hello, Mr. Matheny. Who are your friends?"

Mitch stood up. So did I. "Tell her who we are," he said to me. So he didn't know her. That put her in deep trouble here for sure.

"That's Mr. Mitchell with the beard," I told her. "The beauty who ushered you in is Leo. And this character behind me who has just put away his gun so as not to alarm the ladies, is Brad."

She turned her head to each one as I named them off. "I'm Sheila Glasgow," she said steadily. "May I sit down with you gentlemen?"

She had us all off-balance, and no wonder. Mitch gestured to Leo to pull up another of the terrace chairs for her. "Join the party, by all means, Miss Glasgow," he said courteously. Then, with more iron in his voice, "And tell us what your business is with Mr. Matheny."

We all sat down around the umbrella table.

Leo said, sotto voce, "It's the stewardess off his plane, Mitch."

"Indeed?" said Mitch. "Then I repeat my question."

Sheila Glasgow's eyes went to the blue box in Mitch's hand. "My business isn't only with Mr. Matheny," she said. "It's also with those diamonds."

That shook all of us. This babe not only knew I'd

lifted a package off her plane, she knew what was in it. Mitch came close to gaping at her. Brad pulled in a quick breath. Leo froze.

"Diamonds?" Mitch asked in a neutral voice. "What about them?"

"They're counterfeits," said Miss Glasgow.

That shook us even more. Brad squeaked, "This girl is high on something, Mitch. She needs help. Shall I get her to a doctor?"

Mitch paid no attention to his problem child. He was too interested in the girl. He played it carefully: "I'm afraid you've lost me. How did you arrive at the remarkable conclusion that this box contains diamonds? And even if it did, which I don't for a moment admit, what in the world makes you think they'd be fakes?"

"I didn't say they were fakes. I said they were counterfeits."

"What's the difference?" I asked, getting a black look from Mitch.

She gave me the side of her eyes. "Counterfeits are real diamonds, only they're synthetic. They're man-made."

"So what's the sweat?" Leo said. Practical Leo.

For some reason, I got the impression Miss Glasgow was enjoying herself, maybe because Mitch was listening as closely as any of us. "Synthetics, even perfect ones like those," a finger again indicated Mitch's blue box, "aren't worth as much as real ones, the kind nature makes. Their refractive index is about eight-thousandths less, for one thing."

Mitch pretended sarcasm. "And purely out of curiosity, may I ask what difference the refractive index makes?"

Miss Glasgow permitted herself a small smile. "About

twelve hundred dollars a carat."

Mitch didn't bat an eye. Bad news, I thought. It looked like one of Mitch's subsidiaries might have to report a loss. Miss Glasgow wasn't fooling.

She went on, "I know there are diamonds in that box, Mr. Mitchell. And I know they are counterfeits. So why can't we discuss this like reasonable people?"

"Because I simply do not believe you, Miss Glasgow. And I have trouble being reasonable with liars." It was pleasantly done, but there was a bit of temper in his voice now. He didn't like to be lectured in front of his people, that was sure, and not by a pretty girl who tells him that his diamonds might be worth six figures less than he'd thought.

"I am *not* a liar," she said. "I know there are diamonds in that box because I put them there. And I put the box in the plane seat. And when I put the diamonds in the box, they were counterfeits. So they're *still* counterfeits."

Mitch didn't bluff anymore. Nobody said anything for a minute. Then Mitch made an effort. "They were genuine when they left Europe," he said. "Are you claiming that you switched them in New York for counterfeits?"

"Good thinking, Mr. Mitchell," she said sweetly. I hoped she wouldn't push Mitch too far. He might just give Brad one nod and the next minute it would be *pow!* with the gun and good-bye Miss Glasgow. So ease up, lady . . .

Almost to himself, Mitch muttered, "Then you got to José or Matheny."

"That's right. I got to both of them."

"Not to me," I said. "You didn't get to me."

"Yes, Mr. Matheny, I certainly got to you. By proxy,

over the telephone. And on flight 306 this morning."

"Shut up," Mitch said to me. He was really upset now. "You might have conned Matheny, but you couldn't have got to José. He's seventy years old and hates women."

"He's not seventy years old any longer," Miss Glasgow said. "He's dead."

All this jazz about José and Matheny left me out in the cold. I didn't have the faintest idea what she was talking about. But Mitch and his boys did. They exchanged looks, and Mitch said, with zero sorrow in his voice, "So José's dead. Too bad." He fixed a speculative eye on Glasgow. "Is *that* your angle, Miss Glasgow? Are you bucking for José's job? And holding out the real diamonds to give you leverage for a deal?" There was a hint of admiration in the words, like when he'd complimented me on recovering the package so smoothly the first time.

Another small smile from Miss Glasgow caused a minor miracle in her face. It came alive like poor old José never would again. She said, "No, that's not exactly my angle, Mr. Mitchell. Try another guess." She was going to get herself shot, couldn't she see that?

"Blackmail, then?" Mitch asked, holding out a hand to keep Brad quiet.

"That's closer. Let me put it this way. My angle is simply to make you pay through the nose for smuggling those diamonds. All of you."

A stray breeze moved briefly in the leaves of the trees that grew on the steep hillsides flanking the terrace. Mitch must have been working hard at his rule about not being precipitate. He kept snapping the catch on the blue box of diamonds with a clicking noise like the safety on Brad's gun. It made me want to duck.

Instead, I said, "This kid's a phony, Mr. Mitchell. A rank amateur. What she's trying to do, she happened to see me lift the package off her plane this morning, and she's trying to build it into something big for herself. There's nothing counterfeit about those diamonds, I guarantee it. They're the originals. Or why would *I* have tried for them? Throw this chick out. She's nothing."

Mitch gave me a cold stare. "She came here asking for you," he said. "So she's working with you. That two mouthy strangers in one day should try to muscle in on this same small enterprise, and not be connected in some way, is just too coincidental to believe, Mr. *Matheny*. I suggest that *you* switched the diamonds yourself—if switching took place—in the airport men's room. You planned to disappear with the genuine stones leaving the counterfeits still concealed in the airplane seat, perhaps. We were meant to believe that Matheny had missed the flight for some reason. Only things went wrong for you and Miss Glasgow. Brad and Leo caught up with you before you got away with the diamonds." He gave a smirk that said, "I know how people's minds work."

What he said was close enough to the truth to make me squirm a little, except for the part about the chick. Still, I didn't blame him for thinking she was in on the caper with me. She *had* arrived like the Marines, and thrown them another curve about the diamonds, just when I was in deep trouble with my own little scheme to get Matheny's money. If she was a Marine, she was the prettiest one I ever saw.

She pushed her chair back from the table. "I'm not working with Mr. Matheny," she assured us firmly. "As a matter of fact, I've come to arrest him." She said it so seriously that Mitch and the boys almost busted out laughing. "Along with the rest of you," she finished.

That brought more grins. Since they were convinced she was working with me, *they* were enjoying themselves. Two could live in that little upstairs hideaway as cheaply as one.

Miss Glasgow stood up, turning a little pink. "Don't laugh. I can do it. I'm not really a stewardess, you know."

"What, then?" Mitch was amused.

With an air of triumph, she announced, "Right now, I happen to be a girl who has two sharpshooters with rifles planted in the trees on each side of this terrace, ready to break your heads or your kneecaps if you move a muscle." While we were digesting that one, she gave it a final flourish. "I'm a U.S. Customs inspector on special duty, if you really want to know."

So it hadn't been a breeze on the edges of the terrace. I gave her credit. She'd held us there, gossiping like a sewing circle over brownies and tea, while her men took care of John, whoever he was, downstairs, and positioned themselves on the hillsides to sweep the terrace with their fire. Neat. She ought to feel pretty proud of herself.

But her patriotic announcement fell flat on its face. I believed her, knowing what I knew, but the rest of the boys didn't. Mitch's face split in a grin that wiggled his goatee. "What are we supposed to do? Stand up and salute?"

That irked her a little. "I'd advise you not to stand up unless you want a bullet through your leg."

"Give her to me, Mitch," Brad said. One-track mind.

Miss Glasgow pulled a whistle from her blouse pocket and blew on it. "That'll show you," she said.

I was trying to keep them all under my eye at once,

a tough assignment. I thought I'd figured out why she'd pushed her chair back a minute ago: to be out of the line of fire. I felt naked myself, sitting between Mitch and Brad, because that figured to be right *in* the line of fire.

A man's voice sounded from high on the hillside to the left of the terrace. "Freeze," it said. "This bullet can travel faster than you can move."

The words fell onto the terrace like rocks into a quarry pool, sending ripples of shock clear out to the railing. All in one split second, Mitch and Brad and Leo changed their attitude to Miss Glasgow. I could see it happening by watching their faces. The wise grins went away and flash fear suddenly bit in.

Mitch and Leo and I sat as still as a rasher of corpses, taking no chances with the hidden guns. Brad had a better idea. Like an eel, he slid under the table, clawing at his gun, and flopped over on his belly. It was fast thinking and fast acting. Lying there, the metal tabletop would partially protect him from any cross fire coming from the hillsides above.

He didn't waste his time on unseen targets or any of that shoot-you-in-the-leg stuff, either. He raised the gun in his right hand six inches from the floor, resting on his right elbow, and brought it to bear on Miss Sheila Glasgow's face. There was plenty of room between my legs and Mitch's under the table for him to get her in his sights. In his tenor voice he shouted, "Call them off or you get it first!" She wasn't in any doubt about who he meant.

There was saliva in the corners of his mouth. I wasn't sure he could control himself much longer, since he'd been wanting to shoot somebody all day. So I kicked the gun out of his hand.

It went off as it was jerked from his fingers and

skidded along the terrace floor toward Miss Glasgow. I don't know where the bullet went. Brad snarled like a sick cat and I brought my heel down hard on his wrist under the table. Bones grated and cracked under my shoe. Brad screamed.

Nobody else on the terrace said anything except Miss Glasgow. She yelled, "Hold it, Joe!" in a shaky voice. She was looking just a little scared for such a near miss. She stooped down and came up with Brad's gun. She wasn't familiar with the make, you could tell, but she didn't need to be handy with it now. It was a tableau there on the terrace. Everyone was playing statues as hard as he could. Rifle barrels looking at you when you can't see them are pretty uncomfortable.

I said to Glasgow, "Is it all right for me to move now?"

"No," she said. "I appreciate what you did, Mr. Matheny, but no. Don't move yet." She turned toward the hillside on the left and yelled, "Three of you come in, Joe. Leave Stan to cover the terrace." A regular general for strategy.

I looked down at Brad. He was holding his right wrist in his left hand and groaning. His face was the color of library paste. I said to Miss Glasgow, "He's got another gun."

She flushed and came over and stooped again, lifting my gun out of Brad's hip pocket. He didn't try to stop her. All the starch was out of him. He was ready for a rest.

"That's mine," I said, and casually held out my hand for the gun, but she wasn't having any. She stepped back against the glass wall of the livingroom and waited for Joe.

I thought it was likely Joe was up there on the hillside all alone, and she was bluffing about having four men with her. She held Brad's gun on us nervously until a heavy-set lad walked out on the terrace with a rifle in his hand—and I was wrong. Two other men came climbing over the rail of the terrace from the trees on the right side, also with rifles, and with "police" written all over their faces and feet.

Two of them dragged Brad out from under the table and cuffed his bad wrist to his good one, not trying to be gentle. Their buddy cuffed Leo's right wrist to Mitch's left one. All this took place without a word from anyone except for Brad's groans and a string of salty language that came out of Mitch's mouth like a ribbon unrolling and wasn't meant for mixed company. I was surprised at Mitch. I'd figured him for a gentleman.

Miss Glasgow took the blue box of diamonds from him like candy from a stunned baby. When she could make herself heard over his background cursing, she said to Joe, "That's fine. One more to go. Matheny, here, is also going."

Joe's two followers shoved Leo, Brad and Mitch into the livingroom toward the elevator. Joe started toward me. "Wait a minute," I said. "You don't want me."

"I certainly do," Miss Glasgow said, "whether you helped me with that—that Brad or not."

Helped her! I'd saved her carnation-scented life, if she only knew it.

Joe grabbed my right hand to snap on a cuff. I dipped my left into a camouflaged pocket I have and showed her what I took out of it.

Her eyes got round. She said, "I don't believe it."

"Now who's calling who a liar? It's true." I waved the badge and the ID card at her. "Read it."

She read it. "FBI?" she murmured. Then, stubborn, "No, you're a smuggler."

I said, "Can we talk?"

She finally told Joe to turn me loose and go and get the boys into the cars and tell Stan he could come out of the trees now. Joe went, with a funny look in my direction.

We sat down at the terrace table. I said, "You first, Miss Glasgow. Are you really a Customs girl?"

"Yes, I am. And Sheila to you. Any friend of the FBI is a friend of mine. We eat from the same trough." She smiled at me now. "Should I call you Al?"

"That's my name. So, you first."

She hesitated. "Well, this Mitchell you led us to, he's got to be the head of a big smuggling operation." She gave me a puzzled glance. "I can't understand . . ."

"What put you onto Mitch?"

"You did. That's what I can't believe . . ."

"Forget about me for a minute. How about the diamonds?"

"Maybe I'd better start from the beginning," she said. "We've known a lot of contraband was getting by us at Kennedy International in New York, but we couldn't figure out how it was done exactly, or who was running the stuff in. Then, day before yesterday, we got one of those once-in-a-lifetime breaks. The courier who was bringing those diamonds in from Europe had a heart attack just as he was going through customs inspection at Kennedy. Our inspector helped him until an ambulance arrived."

"The courier was this José you mentioned?"

"Yes, an old man, head of a small export-import firm, we found out." She laughed. "Mostly import, it seems. Anyway, he thought he was dying, which he was, and he kept worrying about a message he had to get to somebody named Matheny in New York." She dimpled a little when she smiled.

"That's me," I said.

"Our inspector promised the courier he'd see to it that Matheny got the message. So what was the message? The old man said he wouldn't know until he heard from somebody named Ruby in TGA's maintenance department, and a lot of other ramblings that didn't make much sense. Our man did get Matheny's telephone number out of José before they took him away."

I nodded. "Boulevard 3-2459."

"Show-off," Sheila said. "On an off chance, our man gave orders for a specially thorough check of the TGA plane José had come in on, and they found the diamonds in José's seat. So then we knew we were on the track of something pretty big, maybe the biggest. And we thought we might use the diamonds to lead us to the top people in the smuggling ring. We confiscated the real diamonds, of course, as contraband, and substituted counterfeits in seat 42."

"Who was this Ruby in TGA maintenance?"

"Ruby Cassavetta, her name is. We found her within an hour after finding the diamonds. We scared her with a smuggling charge and she told us about the system. Somebody, obviously José, cabled her a flight number from Europe every so often. Being in maintenance, she kept track of that particular plane when it landed at Kennedy until it was serviced and ready to return to domestic flights. As soon as she found out what its first domestic flight would be, she let José know, by telephone. She swears that's all she had to do with it. Didn't even know who José was. Just called a certain telephone number and gave the flight information to the man who answered. Never saw anybody connected with the scheme in the flesh."

"How'd they recruit her, then?"

"By telephone," Sheila said. "Somebody, probably

José, propositioned her by telephone, she says, and mailed her money to her."

"When did you come into it?"

"We wanted somebody to keept an eye on seat 42, and for me to fake the stewardess thing seemed the best way to do that. The airline cooperated, of course, and some local law was tipped off to meet the plane and render any assistance I might need."

"You make a pretty fair stewardess," I said. "At least, you smell nice."

"And you, Mr. Matheny, led us right to Mitchell and those two creeps of his. How come? It's your turn now. What were *you* after Mitchell for?"

"We weren't after him for anything. He's just a bonus. We were after Matheny for bank robbery. He and a couple of buddies robbed a bank here in Pittsburgh last month, and a guard got killed in the process, or fatally shot, at least. That was probably our friend Brad, I think. He and Leo fill the bill for Matheny's companions in the knock-over, from the guard's description. He didn't die until after he'd described the robbers to us. Matheny was easy, once we knew the guy who robbed the bank was a man well over six feet tall who threw his left foot. We've had Matheny on our books for fifteen years, more or less. Well, we found Matheny a few days ago, living in a dump in Forest Hills with nothing to do, and before we pulled him in, I thought we ought to take a shot at recovering the ninety thousand he stole from the bank—or some of it —if possible. The dough had to be somewhere, and we thought Matheny would lead us to it."

Then I told her about my side of the thing, about taking the call intended for Matheny. "I suppose that was one of your men, standing in for José?"

"Yes. We hoped he did it near enough like José's

calls to make Matheny follow through."

"I couldn't say about that. But the message was plenty tough enough for *me* to figure out. I almost missed it." I couldn't keep my eyes off her face. "Have you got the New York end cleaned up?"

"Almost, with José dead and Ruby allowed just enough rope to operate normally if anybody should happen to get in touch with her over this diamond smuggling."

"They got in touch with her today," I said. "And she made a liar out of me." I told her about it.

"How about Matheny?" she asked.

"In the slammer," I said. "I gave the word to pull him in after I drew a blank in his room last night. One of our boys who just happened to be passing out religious leaflets nearby made the arrest." I paused. "Where the hell did you get hold of those counterfeit diamonds?" I still thought they were real.

"We confiscated them from a tourist trying to sneak them through customs last year," she said. "Now I have a question."

"Shoot."

"Don't use that word. In this crazy mix-up, have you found any leads to your bank money?"

"I think so," I said. "Mitch has been running a kind of conglomerate here. His word. Smuggling, bank robbery, car theft, maybe gambling. I think Matheny knocked over the bank for Mitch. Mitch planned the job and hid the boys out here in this house till the heat died. And probably kept the money for them, too. It wouldn't surprise me if we find a lot of loot in the elevator." I waved toward the livingroom.

"The elevator?"

"Sure. It has a false back panel, with concealed hinges down one side. I noticed it when they brought me up here. And the cage is too shallow for the size of the shaft. I think Mitch has a big hidey-hole in the back of the elevator. Nifty idea, too. Kind of a free-floating safe, always going up and down from one floor to another. Nobody would ever think of looking for a safe in an elevator."

"Nobody but you," Sheila said tartly.

"Don't be jealous," I said, grinning. "You were too busy to notice elevators."

She turned thoughtful. "They must have smuggled more than diamonds with such an elaborate setup. If there's a safe in the elevator, I bet it'll have more than stolen money and smuggled diamonds in it."

"Sure," I said. "I hinted at that to Mitch. And I thought he reacted."

"If so," Sheila said, "we've *really* done a day's work, haven't we?"

I nodded. I took out a peptic tablet, chewed it and swallowed it.

"What's that?" Sheila asked.

"Never mind. I guess Mitch and his 'people' are in the soup so many ways, they'll never get out."

"It looks that way, doesn't it? My Customs Bureau wants him for smuggling. The FBI wants him for bank robbery. And Narcotics will probably want him even worse than we do."

"To say nothing of the Pittsburgh police. They'll want him for everything from conspiracy to accessory to murder."

"So who's going to get first crack at him?"

I gave it some thought. Then I said, "Look, Sheila, it seems to me we've got a king-size conflict of interest on our hands, among a lot of important government agencies. I, for one, don't want any bad feeling developing between us over a lousy smuggler like Mitch. So I've got a suggestion."

She gave me the smile. "What?"

"I think the only thing to do is for you and me to sit down to dinner together tonight, someplace quiet, and talk the whole thing out. What do you say?"

"Your expense account or mine?"

"I'll toss you for it. Is it a deal?"

"I'd love to, Al," she said, and reached out and touched the back of my hand.

That was good enough for me. As we went to have a look at Mitch's elevator, I made up my mind to one thing. When I took Sheila to dinner, I was sure as hell going to have some gin in my tonic water, heartburn or no heartburn.

THE MAN ON THE HOOK

by Dick Ellis

It was barely nine o'clock when Don Thomas entered the resort hotel lobby. He carried only a small shaving kit, and a newspaper folded under his arm. His eyes were bloodshot and his hand shaky as he signed the register at the desk: *J. D. Jones, Chicago, Ill.*

The desk clerk, who knew a hangover when he saw one, murmured sympathetically, "Dining room's open, Mr. Jones, if you'd care for breakfast. Lots of good hot coffee, perhaps."

Don Thomas grimaced. "Fine. I could use it."

He left his shaving kit at the desk, crossed the lobby and entered the dining room. He took a small table in a corner, as far as possible from the morning sunlight that flooded in through the huge picture window that made up most of the room's east wall. Beyond the window was a green lawn that stretched down to the shore of a sparkling blue lake. Already a few sailboats scudded about the lake in the morning breeze.

Thomas shuddered at the harsh glare of colors. Little men with hammers were pounding away inside his skull, and his scalp still tingled from the ministrations of that barber who had cropped his shaggy brown hair down to its present bristly crew cut an hour ago.

He ordered coffee and toast. He opened his paper, the early edition of the Midwest City *Guardian*. Banner

headlines screamed: REPORTER SOUGHT IN BRU-
TAL MURDER. The drop head carried on: "City
Newspaperman Implicated In Double Slaying."

Don Thomas sent an uneasy glance around the dining room. A good many guests were having breakfast
amid a buzz of conversation and the homely tinkle of
silverware and china. No one appeared to be paying
any attention to him. He gulped coffee and squinted
back to the paper.

The story concerned a young woman and her father who had been murdered the preceding night in
their apartment in Midwest City, some hundred miles
from the lakeside resort. According to the *Guardian*
the case was all but solved; there remained the minor
detail of arresting the killer. With a sort of mourn-
ful outrage, the paper named the suspect—Donald
Thomas, age thirty. For the past year Thomas had
worked as a reporter on the *Guardian*. The paper im-
plied that Thomas' betrayal of the sacred halls of
journalism was almost as bad as the near certainty that
he was a sadistic, ruthless murderer.

The evidence against him was more than damning.
It was known that he had dated the dead girl—Ilene
Levitt, age twenty-five—for several months. Mutual
friends stated that it was an often stormy romance.
Thomas was a heavy drinker, given to violent fits of
temper, and extremely jealous by nature. And Ilene
Levitt had now and again enjoyed dating other men,
much to Thomas' outspoken anger.

"It was a bad situation," friends said. "Ilene should
have broken off with that guy a long time ago."

The previous evening Thomas had brought the girl
home by taxi at approximately ten-thirty. There were
witnesses, other residents of the apartment building
where the girl and her father lived. These witnesses

were sitting in lawn chairs in front of the building, and they not only saw Thomas with Ilene, but also heard a snatch of their conversation as they came up the front walk and entered the building. All agreed that the young couple were engaged in bitter debate.

Ilene was heard to snap, "I tell you, I won't stand any more of it," to which Thomas had retorted, "Yeah? We'll see about that . . ."

One of the witnesses declared that Don Thomas had sounded, "Positively vicious."

The couple had entered the building, and nothing more was seen or heard of them. But it was noted that Thomas did not come out the way he had entered.

At a few minutes before eleven the girl's father arrived: William Levitt, age fifty-six, partner in the prosperous business firm of Levitt and Newer, Inc. The faithful witnesses on the front lawn stated that Levitt was his usual friendly, if rather preoccupied, self. He did express surprise—and some annoyance—when told that his daughter and her young man had come in half an hour before. He abruptly hurried into the building.

Moments later the crack of a shot was heard in the third-floor corridor. Startled neighbors investigated. They found William Levitt sprawled in the open doorway of his apartment, door key still clutched in his dead hand.

And inside the apartment they found Ilene Levitt. She had been brutally beaten and slashed with a knife. The knife, found beside her body, matched a set discovered in the Levitts' kitchen.

So the sequence of events was all too obvious. Donald Thomas had gone into the apartment with Ilene. Between ten-thirty and eleven he had murdered her in a passionate rage. William Levitt had innocently walked into what the *Guardian* called "The gore-spattered murder apartment," and the killer, caught at his grisly work, had shot the father and fled unseen.

There were several ways out of the building, and only the front entrance had been under constant observation.

At press-time, no trace had been found of Donald Thomas, and no photographs of the wanted man had been discovered. He was described as medium size, medium build, with a shock of overlong brown hair, and usually wearing hornrimmed glasses.

However, ironically enough, he was well known to many members of the Midwest City Police Department. For the last six months he had been assigned as the *Guardian's* day-shift police reporter. His arrest was expected momentarily, if not sooner.

Thomas found that his hands were shaking as he folded the paper and placed it on the table beside his plate. He'd read the story earlier, of course, and heard the repeated bulletins on his car radio during the drive from Midwest City to the resort. But there was no getting used to it.

A shadow fell across the table. Thomas looked up with a start. A squat, pudgy man stood there, and for a moment their glances met. Then the man moved on across the dining room toward the door. He wore a hearing aid, its cord running down from his left ear and under the collar of his rumpled, lightweight jacket.

Thomas watched the pudgy man out of sight. The description of himself in the paper would fit half the men in the country, and with his hair trimmed down almost to the bone, and without his glasses, it was possible that even some people who knew him wouldn't recognize him. But he suddenly felt as if there were a large neon sign suspended over his head, complete with a flashing arrow pointing at him, and the words:

"Don Thomas, Wanted For Murder!"

The little men inside his head redoubled their efforts to hammer their way out. For that, at least, he had a cure. Dropping change on the table, he left the dining room, picked up his room key and shaving kit at the desk in the lobby and started for the elevator.

By now the resort was in full swing. Scattered around the lobby were chattering groups—some dressed for a hike into the hills around the lake, others headed for the lake itself, to swim, or sail, or fish, or all three. Everyone seemed determined to have fun. Most were young, but there were a number of older men and women. These Thomas examined with care as he waited for the elevator to return from the hotel's upper regions, but he didn't see the man he'd come here to find.

The elevator came and he rode it up to the fourth floor. He found his room and went inside, locking the door behind him. He stared longingly at the big double bed, but sleep would have to wait.

Unzipping his shaving kit, he dumped its contents on the bed: razor, soap, toothbrush and paste; a heavy silver-cased wristwatch; a snub-nosed .32 pistol; an unopened pint of bourbon.

This last article was what he wanted right now. He opened the bottle, found a glass in the tiny bathroom, and poured a generous four fingers. He downed it in two gulps. When he could breathe again, he poured a second, smaller drink, then firmly recapped the bottle and put it away in a dresser drawer.

By mischance his eyes met his reflection in the mirror above the dresser. He shuddered. With his bristly hair and red-veined eyes, he might be a convict just escaped from a prison work farm—except he didn't look healthy enough.

He wore wrinkled slacks and a wilted, tail-out sports

shirt. He wished he'd been able to go by his place last night and pick up some clothes, but that wouldn't have done at all—not for a murder suspect on the run.

For a moment he thought about Ilene. His face twisted with pain. That silly squabble they'd had last night, and the horror that it had led to. . . . He shook his head violently. He wasn't going to think about that. It led only to self-loathing and sick regret, and those things wouldn't help Ilene—not now.

Nothing would help Ilene; or her father. Thomas had liked William Levitt well enough though the feeling hadn't been mutual. The old man had just two loves in his life—the brokerage business in which he was a partner, and his daughter. For his daughter he'd wanted someone better than a ne'er-do-well newspaperman, and maybe he was right.

It didn't matter anymore.

Don Thomas finished his drink in a gulp. He took a shower and shaved. Then he put his soiled clothing back on. He strapped the heavy watch on his wrist and tucked the pistol under the waistband of his trousers. His shirt concealed the bulge the gun made. As he was buttoning his cuffs there was a tap at the door.

Thomas jumped. "Yeah? Who is it?"

"Message for you, Mr. Jones."

Cautiously he opened the door far enough to see a bellboy standing there with an envelope in his hand. Thomas put a half-dollar in the kid's eager palm, took the envelope, and shut the door.

The message was short: "He's fishing on the far side of the lake. Alone. In boat with outboard motor."

Thomas crumpled the paper and envelope and threw them in a wastebasket. He left the room. It was up to him now, for good or bad, everything—or nothing.

He found that there were boats to rent at a dock a few

hundred yards along the beach from the hotel. He walked out onto the veranda, wincing at the sudden yellow glare of sunlight. Shading his eyes with a palm, he spotted the boat house and dock and headed that way.

And a short, pudgy man wearing a hearing aid stood up from a chair on the veranda and stared thoughtfully after him.

Thomas moved along the sandy beach, avoiding the groups of sunbathers and the laughing men and women running to or from the lake. There were a good many boats out on the wide blue expanse—motorboats, sailing craft, even a few canoes. But as far as Thomas could see, all of these were out for the ride. The fishermen would be in the quiet little inlets and coves along the distant shore.

He reached the dock, and rented a battered, leaky boat with an outboard motor. After several attempts he got the motor started, and putt-putted away from the dock, following the shoreline around the lake.

His eyes were smarting from the glare and the strain of trying to see distant objects. He was very nearsighted, but he didn't want to put on his glasses, not just yet.

It took a good quarter-hour to reach the far shore. There was no beach there; heavily wooded hills plunged right down to the waterline. The shore was notched with coves and occasional inlets where creeks emptied into the lake. And here were the fishermen, alone or in twosomes, their boats at anchor or drifting slowly over the deep blue water, all grimly intent on their business.

Thomas throttled his boat down to a bare crawl. He took his glasses from his shirt pocket and put them on. He had gone perhaps half a mile before he saw the man he wanted—William Levitt's business partner, Francis Newer. He found Newer in a shallow cove shaded by overhanging clumps of willow.

He put his glasses back into his pocket, turned into the cove. He killed his motor, letting the impetus carry him on toward the other boat.

As he approached, Newer cried out angrily and reeled in his line before Thomas' boat could foul it. "Watch what you're doing, you fool!"

Thomas didn't answer until the two boats bumped gently together. Newer fumed. He was a tall, middle-aged man with an angular face glowering under a canvas hat studded with variegated fishing lures.

Thomas said, "Sorry. But I had to see you, Mr. Newer. They told me at the hotel I might find you over here."

"Who the devil are you, and what do you want?"

"I'm a reporter. I wanted to interview you about the murders in Midwest City last night."

Newer's deep-set eyes narrowed. "Do I know you?"

"No, sir, we've never met, but I—"

"There's not a thing I can tell you. All I know is that some maniac named Thomas slaughtered my partner's daughter, then shot Bill when he came in unexpectedly. Terrible thing. *Terrible.*"

Thomas nodded. "Yes, sir. Of course, we know all that. My editor thought you might give us some sidelights. Did you know this Thomas at all?"

"Never saw him," Newer scowled. "Heard of him, from Bill—Mr. Levitt. A drunken bum."

"How did you hear about the crime?"

Newer moved around restlessly. "The Midwest City police called me early this morning. I've been vacationing here the past week. There's nothing whatever I could do in the city, so I decided to stay on until Saturday, as I'd planned. Now if you'll excuse me—"

"What about the business, Mr. Newer? With your

partner dead, surely there are—"

"The business will get along very well for another two days. Besides, what possible interest is that to you?"

Thomas shrugged. He was aware that the older man was studying him with ever-deepening attention. Newer had laid his rod and reel down in the bottom of his boat. Now his right hand was concealed behind his back.

There was no sound except the twittering of birds in the trees on the nearby shore and the soft lap of the water against the boats. Glancing back toward the lake, Thomas saw only an empty expanse of water. The two of them might have been in the middle of some remote virgin wilderness. He put on his glasses.

Newer suddenly brought his hand around. There was a gun in it. "You're Donald Thomas," he said. "No—don't move. I should have known right away, from the newspaper—"

"I look a little different without my glasses," Thomas said, "and with my hair cut."

"Well, I'm sure the police will recognize you quickly enough," Newer snapped nervously. "They want you bad—"

"Yes," Thomas agreed, "but you and I know who really killed those people, don't we, Mr. Newer?"

"What's that supposed to mean?" The gun in Newer's fist was aimed directly at Thomas' sweating face.

"When I took Ilene home last night, I left her at the door of her apartment. But as she went inside, I heard her say, 'Uncle Frank! What're you doing here?' Then she shut the door . . ."

Newer didn't move. The gun didn't waver. Finally he said remotely, "So you heard that, did you?"

Thomas slowly nodded. "Yes I did. Ilene and I had quarreled—a silly thing about her wanting me to quit drinking and settle down. It was nothing. Not really. But it did end with my taking her home early, much earlier than anyone had expected."

Newer gave a sudden bark of laughter. "You think the police would believe that for one minute? The idea's insane. That I would harm that girl—"

"It wasn't the girl you wanted. It was William Levitt you were after. Ilene mentioned that you and her father were having trouble. No, when she came in, you saw a golden chance to make everything look exactly opposite to the way it really was—"

Thomas broke off. He thought Newer was going to fire. Then the older man's finger slackened on the trigger. Thomas managed a shaky breath.

"So you figured it out," Newer said, finally. "Very clever of you, but it won't do any good. I was right here, a hundred miles from the city, last night. Ask anyone around the hotel. Perhaps no one actually saw me from nine o'clock until sometime after midnight, but that's all right. I was out here on the lake, fishing, just as I have been every night for the past week. Ask anyone. I'm a great fisherman. Look at the way I hooked you, Thomas."

"Yeah. You got a hook in me, all right. And even if I wriggled off, you'd still be in the clear, as long as people believe that Ilene was the intended victim."

"That's the general idea." Newer's eyes flicked around the cove, on out to the lake and back. The sides of the two boats scraped gently together.

"I had it figured right, then. I wasn't sure until now," Thomas said warily. "You sneaked off and drove into town to kill your partner, and then she got in your way, a poor kid who never did you the slightest harm."

Newer grimaced. "I'm really sorry about that. I told her so—that it was nothing personal—before I knocked her unconscious. I honestly regret that part of it. But she shouldn't have come in before William got there. I'd made an appointment to see him at eleven . . ."

Thomas slowly rested his hand on the bobbing gunwale of Newer's boat. "Why did you want to kill him?"

"He was getting too close for comfort to finding out certain deals I'd made—not altogether legal deals, but quite profitable to me. But William being William, he would have caused a stink. So I didn't have any choice."

"Too bad about you," Thomas said bitterly.

With a sudden shove, he sent Newer's boat rocking away. Newer dropped his hands for a moment to brace himself against the unexpected movement. The moment was long enough for Thomas to pull the gun from under his shirt. Both men brought up their guns in the same split-second. They glared at each other.

"You want first shot, Newer?"

"Don't be a damn fool—"

"Use it or drop it. Right now!"

Newer abruptly lowered his gun, let it fall to the bottom of the boat. "You don't dare fire. Too many people would hear the shot. All you can do is run—until they catch you. So go ahead, Thomas, run."

"After what you've told me?" He wryly picked up Newer's gun.

Newer grinned. "Who would believe you? A wanted criminal, running for your life. Look at you."

"I do look the part. That was the idea," Thomas said. "This whole business was arranged for this moment, Newer, to get a confession out of you—the newspaper stories, some of which I wrote myself, all of it."

"You're—you're lying."

"The cops never suspected me, Newer. When I left Ilene, I did what any red-blooded newspaperman would do after a quarrel with his girl. I went straight to a bar and got drunk. I was there a quarter of an hour before William Levitt was killed. I had some very good witnesses, including two off-duty cops I know."

Newer scrubbed a hand over his bony face. "It's still my word against yours."

"Not quite. The Midwest City boys arranged to have the sheriff's office in this county plant a deputy out here to help me. There he is now."

Newer gave a startled grunt, jerked his head around to follow Thomas' gesture. A squat, pudgy man was just emerging from the trees down at the end of the cove, about fifty yards away.

"He couldn't possibly have heard," Newer snarled.

Thomas said quietly, "Wave your arms, Deputy."

The man on the shore obligingly waved his arms.

"Amazing what they can do with radio, these days," Don Thomas said. "This watch on my wrist, for instance, is really a miniature transmitter, and the hearing aid the deputy is wearing—that's a receiver, attached to a tape recorder he has in his coat pocket. What's the matter, Mr. Newer? You look sick. Like you'd just swallowed a hook, maybe."

Francis Newer looked more than sick.

"Let's get to shore," Thomas said. "I've never met the deputy there, but I want to shake his hand. And Mr. Newer? Don't take it so hard. There's nothing personal. Nothing personal at all."

ROOM WITH A VIEW

by Hal Dresner

His frail body covered by blankets and cushioned in six of the thickest pillows money could buy, Jacob Bauman watched with disgust as his butler set the bed tray before him and opened the curtains, drenching the room in morning.

"Would you like the windows open, sir?" Charles asked.

"You want I should catch a cold?"

"No, sir. Will there be anything else, sir?"

Jacob shook his head, tucking the napkin into the space between his pajama top and his thin chest. He reached to uncover the breakfast plate, stopped and looked up at Charles who was standing like a sentinel by the window.

"You waiting for a tip?" Jacob inquired sourly.

"No, sir. I am waiting for Miss Nevins. Doctor Holmes said you were not to be left alone at any time, sir."

"Get out, get out," Jacob said. "If I decide to die in the next five minutes, I'll ring for you. You won't miss a thing."

He watched the butler leave, waited until the door closed and then lifted the silver plate cover revealing a single poached egg, looking like a membrane-encased eye, resting on a slice of toast. A miserly pat of marmalade and a cup of pale tea completed the menu.

Ach! Jacob regarded the food with distaste and turned to the window. It was a glorious day outside. The great lawn of the Bauman mansion lay green and even as a billiard cloth, inlaid with the gleaming white gravel of the horseshoe driveway and dotted here and there with small bronze statuary, a flirtatious goddess cloistered in cherubs, a wing-footed messenger, a grim lioness in congress with her cubs; all very hideous but all very expensive. At the left end of the horseshoe, outside the small brick caretaker's cottage, Jacob saw his groundsman, Mr. Coveny, kneeling in examination of an azalea bed; to the right of the driveway, before the prohibitive iron spear gates, the doors of the two story garage were open and Jacob could see his chauffeur polishing the chromium grill of Mrs. Bauman's blue convertible while talking to Miss Nevins, Jacob's young day nurse. Beyond the gate the outer lawn stretched unbroken to the road, a distance so great that not even Jacob's keen eyes could distinguish the passing cars.

Poor Jacob Bauman, Jacob thought. All the good things in life had come too late. Finally, he owned an impressive estate but he was too sick to enjoy it; finally, he was married to a young woman who was beautiful enough to turn any man's head but he was too old to take pleasure from her; and finally, he had gained a shrewd insight into the mysteries of human nature, but he was bedridden and limited to the company of his servants. Poor rich Jacob Bauman, he thought. With all his wealth, luck and wisdom, his world was bounded by the width of his mattress, the length of driveway he could see from his window and the depth of Miss Nevins' mind.

And where was she? He turned to the clock surrounded by bottles, pills and vials on the night table.

Six minutes after nine. Peering out the window again, he saw the girl in the white uniform look at her watch in dismay, blow a kiss to the chauffeur and start walking, hurriedly, toward the house. She was a robust blonde girl who walked with a gay bounce, arms swinging, an exuberance of energy that tired Jacob vicariously. Still, he watched until she disappeared beneath the porch roof and then turned back to his breakfast. She would stop to say good morning to the cook and the maid, he calculated, and that meant he would just be finishing his egg and toast when she knocked.

He was chewing the last dripping crust of toast when the knock came; he called "Go away" and the nurse entered, smiling.

"Good morning, Mr. Bee," she said cheerily. She put her paperbound novel on the dresser, glancing with no special interest at the chart left by the night nurse. "How are you feeling today?"

"Alive," Jacob said.

"Isn't it a terrific day?" the girl said, walking to the window. "I was standing outside talking to Vic before and it's just like spring out. You want me to open the windows for you?"

"I don't. Your doctor friend warned me about getting a chill."

"Oh that's right . . . I forgot. I guess I'm really not a very good nurse, am I?" she smiled.

"You're a nurse," Jacob said. "Better you than the kind that never leaves me alone."

"You're just saying that. I know I'm really not dedicated enough."

"Dedicated? You're a pretty young girl, you've got other interests. I understand. You say to yourself, 'I'll be a nurse for awhile, the work is easy, the food is good. So I'll save some money until I get married.' "

The girl looked surprised. "You know that's just what I said to myself when Doctor Holmes offered me this job. You're very smart, you know that, Mr. Bee?"

"Thank you," Jacob said dryly. "You get old, you get smart." He took a sip of his tea and made a bitter face. "Ach. Terrible. Get this away." He kicked feebly under the covers.

"You really should finish it," the girl said.

"Get it away from me," Jacob said impatiently.

"Sometimes you're just like a little boy."

"So I'm a little boy and you're a little girl. But better we should talk about you." He began to re-arrange his pillows but stopped when the girl came to help him. "Tell me, Frances," he said, his face very close to her, "do you have your husband picked out yet?"

"Mr. Bee. That's a very personal question to ask a girl."

"So I'm asking a personal question. If you can't tell me, who can you tell? Am I going to tell anyone? Is there anyone I could tell? Your specialist-doctor won't even let me have a phone by my bed to call my broker once in a while. Too much strain it would be to hear that I lost a few thousand dollars. He doesn't know I can tell what I make and lose to the penny from the newspapers? . . . So tell me," he smiled confidentially, "what's your lover like?"

"Mr. Bee! A prospective husband is one thing but a lover . . . ?" She plumped the last pillow and crossed to the window chair. "I can't imagine what you must think of me."

Jacob shrugged. "I think you're a nice young girl. But nice girls today are a little different from nice girls fifty years ago. I'm not saying worse or better. I'm just saying different. I understand these things. After all, you're just a few years younger than my wife. I know men like to look at her, so I know they like to look at you, too."

"Oh, but your wife is beautiful. Really. I think she's the most stunning woman I've ever seen."

"Good for her," Jacob said. "So tell me about your lover."

"Well," the girl started, obviously pleased, "it's really not definite yet. I mean, we haven't set the date or anything."

"Yes, you have," Jacob said. "You don't want to tell me because you're afraid I'll fire you before you're ready to leave."

"No, really, Mr. Bauman . . ."

"So you haven't set the day of the week. But the month you've decided on, right?" He waited a moment for contradiction. "Right," he said. "Believe me when I tell you I understand these things. So what month? June?"

"July," the girl said, smiling.

"So shoot me, I'm a month off . . . I won't bother to ask you if he's handsome. I know he is . . . And strong too."

"Yes."

"But gentle."

The girl nodded, beaming.

"That's good," Jacob said. "It's very important to marry a gentle man . . . But not too gentle. The ones that are too gentle let themselves get stepped on. Believe me, I know. I used to be a very gentle man myself and you know where it got me? No place, that's where. So I learned to be different. Not that I still don't make the mistake now and then . . . but every time I do, I pay for it. . . . A bad marriage can be a big mistake, maybe the biggest. You've got to know what kind of package you're getting. But you know, don't you?"

"Yes. He's wonderful. Really, he is. You can't tell, Mr. Bauman, because you don't really know him but if you ever sat down and—" she stopped and bit her lip. "Oh. I didn't mean—"

"So he's someone I know," Jacob said. "Now that's very interesting. I would never have guessed. A friend of mine, maybe?"

"No. No, really, I didn't mean to say that. It just came out wrong. It's not anyone—"

"Doctor Holmes?" Jacob guessed.

"Oh, no!"

"Maybe someone who works for me?" Jacob asked slyly, watching the girl's face. "Charles? . . . No, no. It couldn't be Charles. You don't like Charles very much, do you, Frances? You think he looks down on you, right?"

"Yes," the girl, quite suddenly indignant. "He makes me feel that I'm some kind of a . . . oh I don't know what. Just because he thinks he's so *elegant.* Well if you ask me, he's just a *fish.*"

Jacob chuckled. "You're absolutely right. Charles is a fish. A cold pike . . . But then who could it be? Mr. Coveny is much too old for you so that only leaves . . ." He paused, his eyes bright and teasing, his mouth open. Then he looked past her, out the window, and said, "No, I don't know. Give me a hint. Tell me what business he's in . . . Stocks and bonds, maybe? Oil? Textiles?" His voice rose. *"Transportation?"*

"Oh, you're just teasing me now," the girl said. "You know it's Vic. I bet you knew all the time. I hope you're not mad. Really, I would have told you before but—" A knock on the door interrupted her.

"Go away," Jacob called.

The door opened and Mrs. Bauman, a truly stunning red-haired woman, looking more like twenty than thirty in a daffodil yellow sweater and provocatively tight tan slacks, came in.

"Good morning, all. No, sit down, dear," she said to Frances. "How's our patient this morning?"

"Terrible," Jacob said.

His wife laughed falsely and patted his cheek. "Did you sleep well?"

"No."

"Isn't he horrid?" Mrs. Bauman said to Frances. "I don't know why you put up with him."

"For the money," Jacob said. "Just like you."

Mrs. Bauman forced a laugh. "He's just like a baby, isn't he? Has he had his orange pill yet?"

"Yes," Jacob said.

"No," said Frances. "Is it nine-fifteen already? Oh, I'm—"

"I'm afraid it's almost nine-twenty," Mrs. Bauman said coolly. "Here, I'll do it." She uncapped a vial from the night table and poured a tumbler full of water from a silver pitcher. "Open wide now."

Jacob turned his head from her. "I can still hold a pill and a glass of water," he said. "You don't even *look* like a nurse." He popped the capsule in his mouth and swallowed a sip of water. "Where are you going, dressed up like a college girl?"

"Just into town to do a little shopping."

"Vic has your car all ready," Frances said. "He polished it this morning and it looks just like new."

"I'm sure it does, dear."

"If it's not shiny enough, buy a new one," Jacob said.

"I was thinking of doing just that," his wife countered. "But I thought I'd wait until you're up and around again. Then we'll get one of those little sport cars that only have room for two people and we'll go on long drives together, just the two of us."

"I can't wait," Jacob said.

"My!" said Mrs. Bauman. "Isn't it a marvelous day? Why don't you have Charles open the windows?"

"Because I don't want to get a chill and die," Jacob said. "But thank you for suggesting it."

Smiling tartly, Mrs. Bauman touched her fingers to her lips, then pressed them to her husband's forehead.

"You don't even deserve that much of a kiss today," she said coyly. "If he stays this grouchy," she said to Frances, "don't even talk to him. It'll serve him right." Her smile invited the girl into a woman's conspiracy. "I'll be back early," she said to Jacob.

"I'll be here," he said.

" 'Bye," Mrs. Bauman said cutely and left.

"Close the door," Jacob said to Frances.

"Didn't she look beautiful?" the girl said, crossing the room and then back. "I wish I could wear slacks like that."

"Do your husband a favor and wear them before you get married," Jacob said.

"Oh, Vic wouldn't mind. He hasn't got a jealous bone in his body. He's told me a hundred times how much he likes it when other men look at me."

"And how do you feel about him looking at other women?"

"Oh, I don't mind. I mean, after all, it's only natural, isn't it? And Vic has had—" she colored slightly. "I don't know how we ever got talking about this again. You're really terrible, Mr. Bauman."

"Let an old man have a little pleasure by talking," Jacob said. "So Vic has had a lot of experience with women, has he?"

"Sometimes it's really embarrassing. I mean some

women will just throw themselves at a man. We were at a nightclub two weeks ago Wednesday. On Vic's night off?"

Jacob nodded and again looked past the girl who was starting to talk more rapidly. His wife had just become visible walking across the lawn toward the garage. She moved in a way quite different from Frances, much more slowly, almost lazily. Under the tan slacks her hips rocked, undulating, but just slightly, like a scale seeking its balance. Even the languid swing of her arms seemed to subtly reserve energy, not expend it profligately as Frances did, but rather save the strength, storing it, for the more important motions.

". . . she was really a frightening looking girl," Frances was saying. "I mean, I was actually startled when I saw her come over to our table. Her hair was this jet black and looked like she hadn't combed it for weeks and she had so much lipstick on she must have used up a whole tube getting dressed . . ."

Jacob listened absently, his eyes still on his wife. She had reached the convertible now and stood leaning against the door, talking with Vic. Jacob could see her smile widen as she listened and then, tilting her head back, she laughed. He could not hear the laugh but he recalled it, from years before, as being sharp and light, a stimulating, flattering laugh. Vic, one foot contemptuously propped on the car bumper, thick arms crossed, smiled with her.

". . . really think she must have been drunk," Frances said, fully involved in her story. "I mean I just can't imagine a woman having the nerve to just sit down in a strange man's lap and kiss him. I mean, right in front of his date and all. For all she knew, I could have been his wife."

"So what did Vic do?" Jacob asked, turning from the window.

"Well, nothing. I mean, what could he do? We were in a public place and everything. He just tried to laugh and pretend it was a joke or something. But I couldn't. I mean I tried to, but the girl didn't move and Vic couldn't just push her off. I mean, everyone was watching and I was getting madder and madder and—well to tell you the truth, Mr. Bauman, sometimes I've got a terrible temper. I mean, when it comes to personal things like Vic, I just can't control myself."

"Like with Betty?" Jacob said.

Frances sucked in her lower lip. "I didn't think you knew about that," she said. "I'm really awfully sorry about it, Mr. Bauman, but I just walked into the kitchen to get my lunch and she had her arms around Vic and, well, I guess I saw red."

"So I heard," Jacob said smiling. "I didn't see Betty before she left but Charles told me she wasn't so pretty to look at anymore."

"I guess I did scratch her up terribly," Frances said, lowering her eyes. "I'm really sorry about it. I tried to apologize to her but she wouldn't even listen to me. As if it were all *my* fault."

"And what did you do to the girl in the night club?"

"I pulled her off Vic by her hair," Frances admitted sheepishly. "And if he hadn't stopped me, I probably would have tried to scratch her eyes out, too. I mean, I really went crazy. It was worse than Betty, because she was actually *kissing* Vic. I think if there was a knife or something around, I would have tried to kill her."

"Really?" Jacob said. His look left the girl and returned to the window. Neither his wife nor Vic were in sight then. His eyes scanned the expanse of lawn, passed the statues glinting dully in the sun, to Mr. Coveny who was still probing at the azaleas, and back again, resting on the blazing grill of the convertible. He saw an odd shadow on the car's hood and squinting, defined it as the polishing cloth Vic had been using.

"And how do these little fights affect your feelings about Vic?" he asked casually.

"Oh, they don't. I mean, how could they? It's not his fault that women throw themselves at him. I mean, he certainly doesn't encourage them."

"Of course not," Jacob said. He narrowed his eyes, intently focusing at the dark window above the garage. He thought he had seen a flash of bright yellow there. Or was it just the sun reflecting off the lower pane? No, the window was open; it couldn't have been the sun. There it was again, among moving shadows, a very solid square of bright color, narrowing now and rising slowly, as if it were a piece of fabric, a bright cloth perhaps, being slowly removed from something, someone. And then it was gone and not even the shadows were visible within the frame of the window. Jacob smiled. "I'm sure Vic is very faithful," he said. "If there's anyone at fault, it's definitely the woman. Your jealousy is very understandable. It's only right to fight to hold onto what you have. Even if it means destroying some other part of your life."

Frances looked puzzled. "Do you think that Vic doesn't love me as much because of what happened? He said he understood."

"I'm sure he does," Jacob said. "In fact he probably loves you even more for showing your devotion. Men like things like that . . . No, I was just talking before. Just an old man's talk. After all, what else can I do besides talk?"

"Oh, you could probably do a lot of things," Frances said. "You're very intelligent. I mean, at least *I* think so. You should find a hobby. Crossword puzzles or something. I bet you'd be great at those."

"Maybe I'll try them sometime," Jacob said. "But right now, I think I'll try to sleep for awhile."

"That's a good idea," Frances said. "I brought a new book to read today. I started it on the bus coming over. It's really terriffic, all about this French woman who made a fool of a lot of kings."

"It sounds very good," Jacob said. "But before you start, I'd like you to do me a little favor." He turned and opened the single drawer of his night table. "Now don't be frightened," he cautioned as he withdrew a small gray revolver, "I keep this around in case of burglars. But it's been so long since it's been cleaned that I'm not sure it still works. Would you take it down to Vic and ask him to look it over?"

"Sure," the girl said, rising, taking the gun gingerly. "Hey, it's light. I always thought guns weighed about twenty pounds."

"I think that's a woman's gun," Jacob said. "For women and old men. Now be careful, it's loaded. I'd take out the bullets for you but I'm afraid I don't know very much about those things."

"I'll be careful," Frances said, holding the grip experimentally. "And you try to get some sleep in the meantime. Should I tell Charles to come up while I'm gone?"

"No, don't bother. I'll be fine. You take your time with your fiancé. I think I saw him go upstairs to his room a minute ago."

"He's sleeping," Frances said.

"Why don't you sneak up and surprise him then,"

Jacob said. "He'd probably like that."

"Well, if he doesn't, I'll tell him that it was your idea."

"Yes," Jacob said. "You tell him that it was all my idea."

He smiled, watching the girl leave, then nestled back in the pillows and closed his eyes. It was very quiet and he was so genuinely tired that he felt himself unwillingly starting to doze when the first shot, immediately followed by the second and then a third, sounded across the lawn. He considered sitting up to watch the activity from the window but it seemed like too great an effort. Also, he reasoned, there was nothing he could do, bedridden as he was.

LAST NIGHT'S EVIL
by Jonathan Craig

When I arrived at our house, which is in a rural area some eight miles from the rest of the faculty community, I was not surprised to find that my wife's sports car was not in the garage.

At least she hadn't entertained him—whoever he was —in the house, I reflected as I got back into my own car and restarted the engine. But then, Lucille was a very prudent young woman, as well as a very pretty one and, in the opinion of most of my colleagues, much too young at nineteen to be married to a decidedly unexciting professor twenty-three years her senior.

I'd driven the two hundred and ninety miles from the state capital, where I'd gone to address the State Historical Society, in four hours, slicing my car through the near-zero cold of the December night even faster than I normally drove it. Just before I'd left for the capital, I had been interviewed by the *Riverton Sentinel* on the subject of the town's early myths and legends, and I had been most anxious to get home and read the printed account of the taped interview, which the reporter had assured me would run to a full page. In all honesty, if not modesty, reading my own words in print has always been one of my chief delights.

But my eagerness to read the *Sentinel* was not the major reason for my hurried return from the capital, and after buying a copy of the paper in town I had driven straight home. I had, you see, told my wife that I would remain in the capital overnight, a quite believable lie in view of the bitterly cold weather and the icy conditions on the roads.

Now, at a few minutes past midnight, I knew that the chances were very great that Lucille—or, rather, they—would be in either one of two places: the old slate quarries, or the city dump. Neither spot enjoyed any local popularity as a lover's lane, but both were almost exactly six and a half miles from our house.

When I had first become suspicious that Lucille was seeing someone else during my absences—because I had found lipstickless cigarettes in the ashtray of her car—I had conducted a small experiment. By keeping a careful record of the mileage readings on the odometer of her car, I had discovered that her romantic journeys were invariably of a round-trip distance of thirteen miles. Since the quarries and the city dump were the only two places six and a half miles from our house where one could park a car for any length of time with a reasonable assurance of privacy, the trysting spot seemed almost certain to be one or the other.

As it happened, it was the dump. The tiny white coupe was parked on the frozen ruts midway between a pile of still smoldering garbage on one side and an enormous mound of what appeared to be freshly deposited refuse on the other. A setting not altogether conducive to the tender emotion, it would seem; but then, perhaps very young love was not only blind but lacked a sense of smell as well. In any case, the car was well hidden; anyone not looking for it would not have seen it at all.

I cut my car's engine, coasted the last forty feet,

and got about three yards behind my wife's. They had the engine running for warmth, and the left rear quarter-window was cracked a couple of inches for air.

I had no real plan in mind, but since whatever developed might well entail considerable physical effort on my part, I removed my overcoat, with the anxiously awaited copy of the *Sentinel* in the right-hand pocket, folded it carefully and laid it on the seat. Then I approached the coupe and quietly opened the door on the driver's side.

They were sitting in the raked bucket seats as decorously as one might ask, their heads against the cylindrical headrests—my wife and a rather thin, most unhandsome graduate student whose name, I seemed to recall, was Bolander. Both were sleeping soundly, and the overwarm car smelled strongly of martinis, the latter having unquestionably once resided in the small vacuum bottle which seemed in imminent danger of sliding from my wife's lap. In the pale wash of moonlight, their faces had the untroubled innocence of small children; also like children, they had gone to sleep holding hands.

I stood looking at them for fully half a minute; then I closed the door and leaned an elbow on the top of the car, watching the shredded winter clouds drifting across the face of the moon, as bleak a winter sky as I could remember. No lover's moon, that, I reflected vaguely as I reached for a cigarette; nothing there to inspire the love songs of my own youth; nothing but a cold, disinterested witness to an inconsequential happening in the middle of a smoldering city dump.

Surprisingly, I felt nothing at all. I was cold, but I felt no emotion.

But later, once I got home and settled down in my

chair to read the *Sentinel's* account of my interview, I suddenly fell into such an excess of self-castigation that it was only by a determined and prolonged exercise of will that I was able to dissuade myself from driving back to town for another copy of the paper. I was still very much upset when the phone rang at five a.m.

It was Harry Benson, the Chief of Police, a friend of mine since high school.

A terrible, a tragic thing had happened, he told me. My wife and a young man had taken their lives in a suicide pact at the city dump. They had taken a discarded vacuum-sweeper hose from among the refuse, connected their car's exhaust pipe with a partly opened window, and packed the space around the hose with newspaper. Then they had, apparently, had a few farewell drinks together while they waited for the engine to fill the tiny car with carbon monoxide and death.

When I hung up, I was still very angry with myself. To have carried it off so perfectly, and then to mar it by using the wrong section of the *Sentinel*—the section containing the interview I had been so very anxious to read—was enough, I should think, to upset anyone.

HOW MANY OF THESE DELL BESTSELLERS HAVE YOU READ?

Fiction

1. **THE TAKING OF PELHAM ONE TWO THREE**
   by John Godey $1.75
2. **ELLIE** by Herbert Kastle $1.50
3. **PEOPLE WILL ALWAYS BE KIND** by Wilfrid Sheed $1.50
4. **SHOOT** by Douglas Fairbairn $1.50
5. **A DAY NO PIGS WOULD DIE**
   by Robert Newton Peck $1.25
6. **ELEPHANTS CAN REMEMBER** by Agatha Christie $1.25
7. **TREVAYNE** by Jonathan Ryder $1.50
8. **DUST ON THE SEA** by Edward L. Beach $1.75
9. **THE CAR THIEF** by Theodore Weesner $1.50
10. **THE MORNING AFTER** by Jack B. Weiner $1.50

Non-fiction

1. **AN UNTOLD STORY**
   by Elliott Roosevelt and James Brough $1.75
2. **QUEEN VICTORIA** by Cecil Woodham-Smith $1.75
3. **GOING DOWN WITH JANIS**
   by Peggy Caserta & Dan Knapp $1.50
4. **SOLDIER** by Anthony B. Herbert $1.75
5. **THE WATER IS WIDE** by Pat Conroy $1.50
6. **THE GREAT EXECUTIVE DREAM** by Robert Heller $1.75
7. **TARGET BLUE** by Robert Daley $1.75
8. **MEAT ON THE HOOF** by Gary Shaw $1.50
9. **MARJOE** by Stephen S. Gaines $1.50
10. **LUCY** by Joe Morella & Edward Z. Epstein $1.50